W9-BOK-412

HIS NAME WAS DAVID

HIS NAME WAS DAVID

THE REMARKABLE LIFE OF DR. DAVID PAULSON, MAN OF FAITH AND FOUNDER OF HINSDALE SANITARIUM

By Caroline Louise Clough

REVIEW AND HERALD PUBLISHING ASSOCIATION

WASHINGTON, D.C.

OFFSET IN THE U.S.A.

Table of Contents

DEDICATED

to my sister, Dr. Mary Paulson, who worked shoulder to shoulder with her husband, Dr. David Paulson, in building a monument of faith to the healing power of the Great Physician.

David Paulson, M.D., founder of Hinsdale Sanitarium.

Introduction

At the urgent request of the many friends of Dr. David Paulson after his death in 1916, a book was published entitled *Footprints of Faith,* which in his own words presented the story of the high points of his life of faith and endeavor in the field of medical missionary activity. The edition was soon exhausted.

Today, many years later, with the memory of his influence ever widening, it has seemed opportune to retell the story of his life. In doing so the purpose is not so much to record biographical events as to portray Dr. Paulson's philosophy of life —his simple faith in God—the way he met life's exigencies and conquered them through prayer and trust in his Maker, for these were the things that made him great.

When I was his secretary I was present at most of his lectures, from popular health talks and large Chautauqua appointments down to the more intimate classes of nurses and helpers. Hence this book reflects David Paulson as he was—even his own words, which I have copied from his notes.

Dr. Paulson used simple illustrations—right to the point—with but few unnecessary words, yet whenever it was announced that he was to give a lecture, people flocked to hear him, and filled the house.

Those who knew David Paulson and came under the spell of his remarkable life of faith and prayer, will be inspired again as they read this book. Those who never met this man of God, however little or much they may have accomplished in life, as they trace his footprints of faith will find a longing for a deeper spiritual experience and more power, more faith in God.

The most striking characteristic of his great mind was perseverance under trying difficulties, and when convinced that he was on the side of truth and right he did not fear to stand and act alone.

In this book we endeavor to follow him through his early experiences in gaining an education in Battle Creek, Michigan, down to the heart of needy Chicago, where his faith was severely tested at every turn of the road. His later career at Hinsdale, a suburb of Chicago, reveals to us that all the previous tests of his faith were mere steppingstones to prepare him for the great task of building a sanitarium entirely by faith.

The story of Hinsdale appears in this book quite in detail. Without it Dr. Paulson's life could not be truthfully written. The famous sanitarium in Hinsdale, which Dr. Paulson built through prayer and tears, is now replaced by a much larger modern building at a cost of $3,500,000. The career of this man of God gives illumination to the truth of Longfellow's oft-quoted lines:

"Lives of great men all remind us
We can make our lives sublime,
And departing leave behind us
Footprints on the sands of time;

"Footprints, that perhaps another,
Sailing o'er life's solemn main,
A forlorn and shipwrecked brother,
Seeing, shall take heart again."

Authors never write a book alone, yet the title page usually gives but one name. Many have contributed in various ways to the making of this book. In making particular mention of my literary counselor, Katharine Finn Bee, of Los Angeles, California, instructor in creative writing, I must also gratefully acknowledge my debt to all who have rendered assistance.

—THE AUTHOR

CHAPTER ONE

A Boy's Vow to God

David Paulson was a mere youth, not yet twenty-one, when I first met him. He had finished one year in college—one year removed from the rigors of Western prairie life. No doubt he had lost some of his frontier appearance during that year; still he had a rough, countrified look when I first saw him, giving little promise of the eminent physician and spiritual leader he came later to be.

It was in September, 1889, that my sister Mamie Wild and I left our home in New York for Battle Creek, Michigan. We hoped to continue our education in a Christian school, the Battle Creek College. She was seventeen and ready to enter college. I was younger, and entered one of the lower grades, all in the same building.

To earn our way through school we were to work part time for our board and room at the Battle Creek Sanitarium, the famous health resort across the street from the college. The day we arrived at the sanitarium we were taken to a room on one of the upper floors of the hospital building, to remain there until we could be located permanently. My sister Mamie stepped out of the room and I proceeded to freshen up from our long ride on the train. I was reaching for my fine-checked blue gingham in our bag when a knock came

The old Battle Creek Sanitarium. Destroyed by fire, February, 1902.

on the door and immediately a lanky, six-foot, rather pale-faced fellow trudged in, bent under our large box trunk on his back. He dropped it in a hurry and rushed out of the room. The unceremonious porter was David Paulson, and it was my first introduction to him.

One of the boys in school when David arrived reminded me years later that "David was a crude, unpolished product of a Midwestern farm, not promising to look at. He appeared in school in his homespun suit, with his trouser legs and coat sleeves outgrown by several inches." That schoolboy, who later became the well-known Dr. Daniel H. Kress, was David's classmate through his college and medical school days. He told me further that David was different from most boys—he prayed, and had a purpose in life, and nobody could change him from that purpose. "David," said Dr. Kress, "applied himself to study—he studied while others played."

One of the boys standing by at the time David arrived from his Dakota home said, "Say, if they can do anything with that fellow, the day of miracles isn't past."

I shall never forget the first time I heard him talk. His speech was rapid fire, with a touch of Danish accent. His appearance—well, he must have appeared in college like a package from a country store would seem to us today—wrapped in string and brown paper—yet when talking with him one never thought of his clothes.

There was something in him—a quality of character and a determination to reach his goal—that was unusual for a boy of twenty. The outward appearance does not always give us the true value of a man. One writer says, "We must see the lark within the songless egg." Little did I know then that one day he would be a great man and that I would be his private secretary.

"I grew up on the Western plains," I heard him say many times. That was in the rugged prairie country of South Dakota. His father hired him out to herd cattle. During the summer he tramped the range in his bare feet and would be gone from home for days at a time.

He wanted a pony like the other boys had, but his father, a frugal and industrious man, said they couldn't afford one. To travel over the rough ground and stubble for miles every day with blistered and bleeding feet was more than a ten-year-old boy could endure. "I'm going to pray for a pony," he said aloud one day when only the cattle could hear. He prayed and prayed and kept on praying. One day at home he saw a man with a pony coming up the road. "There comes my pony—there's my pony—the Lord is answering my prayer," he cried. But the man with the pony went right on past.

It was several years before he got his pony. He decided that the Lord had something else in mind for him. "The muscles in my legs are almost as hard as wood," I heard him say once. "I developed them chasing cattle barefooted. If the Lord had answered my prayer, the pony would have had the muscle and I would have been a weakling."

It was through these simple incidents in life that he learned to trust God fully. In telling this experience to an audience one day he said, "The reason some of you have not had your prayers answered is because you are praying for ponies—praying for something to make life more comfortable for yourself. If it doesn't come, don't feel the Lord has forsaken you."

Continuing his lecture on prayer, he said, "I early had an introduction to this question of prayer. When I was a boy eight years old I lost my jackknife, which was a more serious matter for me then than to lose an automobile now even if I had one. I asked the Lord to help me find my jackknife, and He did. So I got a start as a mere youngster in reference to prayer.

"I have traveled far and near, have mingled in a confidential way with thousands of people, and I believe there are but few who have gotten out of prayer all that they might. They say prayers to God, but they do not *pray* to God. He seems too far off. Those of you who have stood on the outer edge of that experience, I want you to know there is something better for you."

He referred his audience to the experience of Moses —a graduate from the University of Egypt, also from the highest military academy in the world. Moses must have been disappointed when he had to herd sheep in the wilderness for years and years just as he was ready to take a high position in Egypt, next to King Pharoah. One day out in the desert wastes he saw a burning bush—he watched it—it was not consumed.

"As he drew near, the Lord spoke to him out of the bush and commanded him to go back to Egypt and deliver his people from slavery. In that burning bush he saw a great mission for his life. It put character into him. It made him the leader of a greater nation than Egypt. The Lord can take the most grievous disappointment in your life, as He did in Moses' life, and through it show you a burning bush of opportunity," he said.

No doubt David was just as full of pranks and fun as any six-year-old boy when his father moved his family from Raymond, Wisconsin, to Beresford, South Dakota. There the father built a sod house, and they became a real pioneer family, commanding the respect of the other settlers far and near.

Being the middle son of five boys, David, according to their young sister Louise, was the victim of all their pranks. No doubt there were a few times when he deserved punishment with the rest, but Louise said it seemed that when the score was settled with Father, David usually got the lion's share of the punishment. There was one exception that she could remember.

The boys made a flatboat and floated it down the irrigation ditch when the water was high, then out into the surging Vermillion River. Their handmade barge upset, spilling them all into the water. Managing to get ashore, all five boys came trudging home in their wet clothes—a long ten miles—only to get nicely warmed by their irate father, who dealt out punishment to all alike.

Church privileges were meager in a frontier town of twelve families, but they lived in the days when camp meetings were popular. For the six Paulson children camp meeting was the one great event of the year. Days and weeks were spent in preparation. The old covered wagon was hauled out, dusted off and greased, then packed for two weeks of camping. Bedding and clothing were prepared, food was cooked, bread baked, and everything neatly packed away in the wagon. They were ready for the thirty-mile, three-day trip to Sioux Falls, site of the campgrounds.

The program at camp meeting was strenuous, lasting from six in the morning to nine at night. There were morning prayers, Bible studies, experience meetings, sermons, evangelistic and revival services.

The children were not neglected, although their training was not so well organized as it is today. They had nature studies, romps on the playgrounds near by, a story hour each day, talks illustrated with colored pictures showing Bible characters, and gospel messages by prominent evangelists who presented the story of Christ in simple language. Even though the activities were strenuous, David earnestly absorbed everything he saw and heard.

It was at one of these camp meetings that David's heart was touched. He wanted to serve the Lord. Although only eight years old, he was baptized. Two years later his mother passed away.

When David was in his middle teens diphtheria struck terror to the neighborhood. Children were dying, and his home was not excepted. He himself was critically ill. I heard him tell that heartbreaking story many times. He said, "I heard my father say to my oldest brother, 'Martin is dead. You must help me carry him out.' I was terribly sick, but I knew they were carrying my brother out of the house to bury him. Soon I heard them come back, and my father whispered to Nels, my brother, 'David will be next. He can't last long. I think we had better wait and bury both boys at once.' "

It was then David began to think seriously about what his life had been. Was he prepared to meet his Maker? Had he anything to make right with his brothers? and his little sister? How about the neighbors? Was there something he must see them about?

As he lay there on his bed, scarcely able to breathe, he asked the Lord to help him right the wrongs he had done. He said, "Dear Lord, I will give you everything—all my life—if you'll let me live." Then he vowed to God that if He would restore him to health, he would give all his life to helping sick and suffering humanity and to working for the salvation of souls. To the surprise of the entire community, the Lord heard and answered that prayer.

David began to breathe with less effort, and it was not long before he was entirely recovered. "I might as well have tried to make a plank reach across the Atlantic Ocean," he said, "as to expect the faith I had in Christ to tide me over the gulf I was facing then." He felt that in some way he had missed the real thing in his Christian experience. In keeping with his vow he proceeded to make everything right with everyone he had wronged.

Sometimes he would use that experience in his public lectures to emphasize some point he was making. One time I heard him tell this: "It takes courage to straighten out your own life so the Lord can answer your prayer for others. I remember I had a row with an Irish woman. I had to get matters fixed up with her. She lived near us. We had some words. She was a woman of action as well as of words. She jabbed a pitchfork into my ankle; then I said some more things—it left a bad spirit. I had to go and ask her to forgive me. I had a lot of other things to do. I had to see a boy whose eye I had blackened in school."

Then he made some observations: "These things have to be done before the Lord can answer our prayers.

I hope the Lord will save me from ever taking any position that will result in leading a human soul away from God. From that moment I took God in as my partner," he said. From then on David's life was never the same. "All that has come into my life that has been sweet, and all I have been able to do, has come and has been done as a result of that sickness and my promise to my Maker," he often remarked.

Another statement he made bears repeating here. He said, "Through all the ages God has never discovered anything better than trouble and affliction to burn the dross out of the soul. That is why His children have always had such a big dose of it. God is fitting them for heaven."

From then on he knew that he must have an education, but how and where was the problem. He had finished the grade school in his small prairie town of Beresford and had attended school in Vermillion twenty miles away, but what next?

CHAPTER TWO

Hard Knocks

David found it was a slow tedious task to save money for his education. He was still herding cattle, but his father took charge of most of his money. To save a quarter here and a dollar there was what he did religiously, thinking only of his goal—getting adequate schooling.

After years of hard work he determined to start for college. During those years he had seen his father laid away to rest, leaving him an orphan.

The time came for the great adventure of his life. He had been accepted at the Battle Creek College in Michigan, which was recommended to him as a good Christian school.

To his surprise, and in answer to his prayers, his eldest brother Nels, who took charge of the family after his father's death, came to David one day and said, "David, I want to have a talk with you." Nels's face was grim. Letting David start for school with but little money had troubled him. "Must I give him more money?" kept racing through his mind. David stood expectant, almost trembling, praying the Lord not to let his brother keep him from going to school.

"It seems you are determined to go to the Battle Creek College, David."

"Yes, Nels, I have settled it. I am going whether I have enough money or not. You can't stop me now."

"I don't want to stop you, David. I just want to know how much money you have toward the year's expenses."

"Well, I can pay for my train fare and possibly my tuition and books. That's about all, but I can work."

"Well, David, I think I had better not let you go with so little money."

"Oh, I can make it. I'll do anything to earn my way," David replied, while his knees shook.

"You had better take this," said Nels, as he produced a roll of well-worn greenbacks from his pocket and with a forced smile handed it to David.

"Oh, Nels, I didn't expect anything like this! Do you mean to give me all of it?"

"Yes, all of it."

"Why, I'll make this do for the entire school year. You've answered my prayer, Nels, and I thank you."

"Well, David, I'm glad you can go, and I wish you success."

Early in September in 1888, with his small canvas telescope bag in one hand, the other grasping the money in his pocket, David Paulson rushed off for the train, a happy lad near twenty, thankful to God for answering his prayers. The little train jerked along over the Midwestern prairies, bringing him to Battle Creek, Michigan, and the college. Now he could work out the dream for his life and fulfill his vow to God.

He advanced rapidly in school, making up the subjects he lacked to enter college along with the first-year students.

The old Battle Creek College. Established 1874.

Summer came. David went to work at the Battle Creek Sanitarium, continuing there until he finished his entire premedical course.

He worked hard that second year—cleaned rooms, beat and tacked down carpets, scrubbed floors, washed windows, washed tinware in the basement, and delivered hot water to the patients' rooms early every morning. (In 1889 private bathrooms or even hot and cold running water in the rooms were scarcely heard of in hotels and institutions anywhere.) He did a hundred and one other things a boy naturally dislikes to do.

When asked to work on the call force, he put all his energy into running calls. The other boys relaxed. "Paulson likes to work, let him do it. He can run all the calls," they said. He usually did.

When he was transferred to the housekeeping department, working for the matron, he had the same experience. When the matron left the room the boys would slacken their work, but David kept right on. They would joke about it, and in a jesting mood say, "Paulson, why don't you stop working so hard, the matron's gone?"

To which he would say, "I'm not working for Mrs. Hall, I'm working for the Lord."

"But you act as though you were the manager."

"I feel like one," was his retort. David couldn't understand why the other boys never seemed to have the same feeling of responsibility he had.

Years later, when he was traveling up and down the country presenting the gospel for both soul and body to large audiences, he met one of those boys. In a Western city a man who looked down at the heel, discouraged with life, came to him and said, "Do you remember me, Dr. Paulson? We used to work together for Mrs. Hall in the old Battle Creek Sanitarium."

"Yes, I remember, Elmer. What are you doing here?"

"Well, I've had a hard time, David. Work is scarce these days. Right now I'm raising chickens for a living on a small place out in the country. I manage to keep the wolf from the door, and that's about all."

Elmer may have been the boy who told Dr. Paulson years before to stop working so hard when the matron was gone. As David looked at him he thought, "This poor fellow! The picture of despair—trying to make a living for his family by raising a few chickens. He had the same opportunities to get an education and to climb to the top as I and all those boys did, yet for some reason he failed."

"Raising a few chickens for a living" came to be in David's mind a symbol of failure in life for those who had been trained for greater responsibilities. In my memory I can see him today trying earnestly to inspire his students with the great principles of medical missionary service.

He said, "You are fortunate to be placed where you can receive this valuable training under experienced teachers. What are you going to do with it? Are you going to be a real help to humanity, or are you going off to some remote spot and raise chickens for a living?"

Then he continued, "Set a goal for your life, and then follow it like the ocean liner, which has the power within itself to plow a straight course through the sea, not like the sailboat, dependent on which way the wind blows. Your parents or your friends may stand like a rock for God's principles, yet that will never save you unless you can get those principles into your own soul."

It was not an easy path David Paulson had cut out for himself. There were plenty of hard knocks in the way. He knew there would be more difficulties ahead, yet nothing could stop him short of his goal.

CHAPTER THREE

David Tells How to Study

David Paulson was working five hours a day at the sanitarium for his board and room. There was no exchange of money for this service. Funds for all other expenses, including tuition and books, he earned through the summer months.

My sister, Mamie, and I were also earning our way through school. Our first job when we arrived was to wait on tables in the patients' dining room. That meant three hours each day. The other two hours my sister worked at odd jobs. I was sent to the laundry to iron.

Some of the boy students waited on tables, but I never saw David there only as he would appear in the serving room after a meal with his basket to pick up scraps for the dog and the bear he had to feed each day. Sometimes I would see him with a load of carpets on his shoulder, following the housekeeper, or in the attic over the laundry, making mattresses.

One afternoon I was sent to the attic to tie a comforter. David was there making a mattress.

"Did Mamie come over to iron?" he asked.

"No. I don't know where she is working this afternoon."

"It doesn't matter, only I thought possibly she ironed for two hours each afternoon now."

"Well, I think you had better keep closer tab on what she does." David blushed, and I knew I had better change the subject.

"Oh!" I said, observing a book lying open in front of him. "I see you're studying while you work."

"Yes, I am. I find there are not enough hours in a day to get everything done, so I double up by studying and working at the same time."

"How can you do that? I can't. I have to keep my mind on my work."

"I had the same trouble, but I trained myself to do it, and now I find it easier."

"Do you always carry a book around with you?"

"Always. If I'm going up or down on the elevator, I whip out my book."

"How can you read on the elevator?"

"Oh, I just catch a line or two, then think about it until it is fixed in my mind. I have to improve every minute."

"It's marvelous what you can do."

"Well, I have noticed that most of the students around here don't combine study with their work. When they begin to work, they stop studying—when they study—no work."

"But you do both."

"Yes; I have learned to do both at the same time."

"Perhaps if we followed your example we might get ahead faster."

"Possibly so. I know *I* have to study this way."

If he studied as fast as he talked, I was sure he would get ahead. I couldn't begin to catch all he said that afternoon.

All the students had a heavy program, but David seemed to take his work more seriously than we did. It must have been that vow he had made to God when he was a boy that spurred him on. Later David was promoted to the job of night watchman. That gave him an opportunity to study between his rounds.

One day many years later he was talking to the nurses in training. I was present to take down his speech. Some of the students came to class without having studied their lessons, giving the excuse that they had no time when working eight hours a day. With a mischievous twinkle in his eye, he said, "Take your textbook to bed with you and sleep with it under your pillow." Then he gave them a worth-while lecture on his philosophy of life as a hard-working student.

He said, "If you think you are compelled to work your fingernails off to get an education, instead of murmuring at your lot, thank the Lord for the opportunity. When I was getting an education I envied the boys and girls who didn't have to work their way through school. Now my heart aches for at least some of them."

David early learned the value of time and how to improve it, which lesson helped greatly to advance him in his struggles toward success. He said in the same connection, "This habit has been of priceless value to me. It enables me to do about the same amount of study each year as I did when I went to college, and that without slighting any of the ordinary duties that life has brought to me."

He felt that the man who does not learn to combine study with work will soon forget nine tenths of what he learns and be left behind in life's struggles.

He said that many discouraged persons are ready to say, "If only I knew how to study, or at least were able to recall what I have studied, I would feel encouraged, but my mind is like a sieve. I feel I shall never amount to anything."

The doctor then asked the students whether they had difficulty in remembering some great calamity that had befallen them—when their house burned down, or when a member of the family was accidently killed. Of course they remembered all the shocking details of such experiences.

"You may say," he continued, " 'Oh, but that is different.' No, it is not different. It requires the same kind of memory to recall such things as is needed to remember what you see, read, and hear. The only difference is that such events make a vivid impression on your mind, whereas you have failed to learn the valuable secret of making what you regard as ordinary things impress you in a similar manner.

"When we get down to the root of the matter there is nothing ordinary in the world. Every act of our lives is full of reality. Every opportunity we have of looking into a book ought to change us for time and for eternity."

Dr. Paulson taught us that the great secret of remembering what is studied is the ability to concentrate the mind fully upon it, shutting out everything else for the time being. Then a definite picture of what is read is made on the mind. "We should never read or study anything that is not worth focusing our attention upon." He said, "You can study even the truth and get so muddled and confused that it will seem tame and uninteresting, or you can so study that it will fall from your lips clear cut and beautifully expressed, fascinating to all who hear."

David Paulson was so absorbed in preparing for his chosen lifework that everything else was secondary—even romance—until on one of those college days when he was nearing his twenty-second birthday an incident occurred that changed his point of view, at least we thought so.

One night my sister came home to our room, her blue-gray eyes dancing. She said, "What do you think happened to me today?"

"I don't know. What did happen?"

"Mrs. Hall gave me a job washing windows on the inside."

"What of that, Mamie? I wouldn't get excited over that."

"Yes you would if the boy you liked was washing them on the outside at the same time," she smiled.

"Of all things, Mamie. Who is the boy? Or do you want me to tell you? I think I can."

"Why, he's David Paulson, of course."

"David Paulson! Well, I'm not surprised, but why do you like him? His English is broken and he talks so fast he is hard to understand."

"You're right there, Carrie. Looks as if you'd never care for him."

"I'm not sure of that, Mamie, but he looks so rough and countrified."

"Don't you see anything in him but his looks, Carrie? He may be a diamond in the rough for all you know."

Mary Paulson Neil, M.D., organizer of Hinsdale School of Nursing.

"I hope you're right, Sis."

"You said his language is broken. That's right. But for your information, Carrie, although David's parents did come from Denmark, he was born in Raymond, Wisconsin."

There was nothing more for me to say.

Just a few days later during study hour in the chapel, a note was secretly passed along from one desk to another until it reached the furthermost desk by the wall, where my sister was sitting. I sat only two or three seats away and saw the message relayed to her. I thought it must have been from David because she was blushing and turning this way and that to make sure no one was watching her, then down again at the note. The tears came to her eyes as she read, "Can you meet me tonight at eight on the sanitarium lawn?" It was signed "David." She showed me the note later.

A large shaded lawn dotted with flowers and shrubbery bordered the sanitarium, but on the front lawn were all kinds of comfortable seats and hammocks, which the patients enjoyed during the day and the young folks at night.

When Mamie read that note she had no thought of the disappointment that was to come. When school was dismissed she met David in the hall.

"Oh, David, I got your note," she smiled.

"What note do you mean? I haven't sent you any note," he blurted.

"Oh," she said with a look of chagrin. "Why, er—here it is, David," and she handed him the penciled message.

"That's not mine at all," he said, shaking his head.

"Of all things! Someone has played a joke on us." Mamie began to realize the full import of that note as she exclaimed, "Oh, I'm sure I know who did it. None other than my friend Peg."

"Peg," he frowned.

"Yes, sir, that was Peg. She's too clever for anything."

"Possibly so," said David, as the look of bewilderment vanished. "Isn't she the girl who brought a live mouse to school one day with a long string tied to it and let it run around the chapel?"

"Yes, that's Peg. I was in the chapel at the time."

"I wasn't, but I heard about it."

"When she saw the monitor coming she dropped the string and let the mouse go free. She got by, too, without being reprimanded," she grinned.

"Evidently she is clever enough to play a trick like this on us," he said as he abruptly turned and went on his way.

It was embarrassing to both of them, but it served to bring those two young people closer together. After that they found time for many "chance meetings on purpose," as our professor was always reminding us.

Both David and Mamie were looking toward careers in medicine, sharing a desire for training in preparation for service to sick humanity. David was almost twenty-two; Mamie had passed her eighteenth birthday.

Years later, when David Paulson, under God, had built a large sanitarium in Hinsdale, near Chicago, I remember hearing him tell his nurses in training, "You must keep your affections in cold storage while taking the nurses' course." He still held to his early belief that his lifework must come first. His budding romance did not deter him from his serious ambition in life. He was always "on duty" for God, whether pulling a patient out of an apparently hopeless condition or teaching his nurses how to study.

It was his years in school—his contacts with medical work and sick patients at the Battle Creek Sanitarium—that deepened David Paulson's desire for a medical career. There was always the one obstacle—lack of means. What should he do? He had already gained experience in the efficacy of prayer. Why not ask the Lord to open the way for him?

CHAPTER FOUR

Discovering the Needs of Humanity

David Paulson, a thinner lad who looked even taller than before, emerged from those years of incessant toil and unceasing study to present himself for graduation in 1890. He had taken but few moments for relaxation in those two years in college; now came the reward. He was handed a diploma that qualified him for admittance into medical school.

As he studied the life of Christ on earth he discovered that physical healing in many cases was dependent on healing of the soul. He felt impelled to combine the ministry of salvation with the gospel of health. He looked to Christ as his example and coupled the spiritual with the physical healing.

He continued to pray for help for his medical training, feeling confident that the Lord would take care of him. His prayers again were answered. He said, "The Lord raised up some folks to lend me the money."

David Paulson was one of twelve graduates from the Battle Creek College who entered the University of Michigan in the fall of 1890. A large house was rented in Ann Arbor, Michigan, where the entire group resided. Daniel Kress and his wife Lauretta, both older than the other students, were in charge.

Howard Rand, David's roommate, soon discovered that David seemed to lack interest in his personal belongings. His thoughts were only for his studies. So Howard took upon himself the task of seeing that David and his belongings stayed together.

Dr. Kress told me years after of one experience of those days that revealed one of David's characteristics. He said, "Many times Howard would come home bringing something David had left behind. One night he appeared with David's hat in his hand. We were amused about it and had our little joke over David's shortcomings. Howard said he was looking around in the lecture room when he noticed David's hat. Not finding its owner, he brought the hat home. Soon David appeared, hatless, books under his arm, and a woebegone look on his face as though he had lost his last friend. He *had* lost his last and only hat, which seemed of great importance to him."

"Well, Dr. Kress," I remarked, "I fancy that hat was no doubt one loss that made a deep impression on his mind."

"Yes, that was true, Caroline. Where do you think he was?"

"I have no idea. Where was he?"

"He was in the professor's office all that time getting some points of the lecture more clearly fixed in his mind."

"That was like David all right, always concentrating on his studies—no room or place for the non-essentials. Sometimes I felt he had trained himself to put ordinary things out of his mind entirely that he might accomplish the one great task he set for himself."

In speaking of his medical training, Dr. Paulson afterward said, "Providence opened splendid opportunities for me; in fact, some of the best medical instruction that was obtainable in those days. Some of these opportunities I know came directly in answer to my prayers."

PAINTING BY GABRIEL MAX

The healing touch of the Great Physician.

He recognized the hand of God at work for him and was thankful he had taken God in as his partner when a mere lad on a sickbed.

Although David's studies in Ann Arbor seemed to transcend all other interests, his heart was in Battle Creek, and he occasionally found a way to span the intervening eighty miles for an evening with Mamie. Their favorite rendezvous was along the banks of the Kalamazoo River. One night as they were by the bridge Mamie said, "David, I wonder why I'm so fond of this river." They had strolled out to the middle of the bridge by that time.

"I can tell you why, my dear. It's because it shows more activity than the deep, quiet streams."

"You must be right, David. It's like life, isn't it?"

"Yes, it is. You see at this point and for miles above stream the Kalamazoo River has many obstacles to surmount. You remember the time a party of us rode down to Augusta? We kept dodging big stones and stumps of trees and other debris, and once our boat nearly upset and I was thrown into the water."

"I certainly do remember that, but we had a nice time that day."

"I learned some lessons from that experience."

"No doubt you did. But look, David, the river is sparkling in the moonlight like a million stars."

"Mamie dear, this river is like life. What if our lives grew to be like this river, with big rocks and boulders of difficulties and persecution to obstruct our path? If that should be true, are you willing to trust the Lord all the way with me?"

"I'm ready and more than willing, David."

There they stood on the bridge—she in his arms, dressed in her soft-blue gown that he admired, with a paisley shawl thrown over her arm. Looking down at her with a heart full of love, holding her hand in his, he said, "Mamie, I wish you would sing Longfellow's song 'The Bridge at Midnight.' "

"You mean to sing it here, right now?"

"Yes, why not right now?"

"All right, David, I'll try it," So Mamie in her clear, strong voice sang:

> "I stood on the bridge at midnight,
> As the clocks were striking the hour,
> And the moon rose over the city,
> Behind the dark church tower."

"Oh, that inspires me," he said as he caressed her hand. "Listen, Mamie, the clock is striking twelve this minute."

"Oh, David, you did that on purpose. How clever you are! But I love you."

"Now, dear, don't lose your head. Remember we have months and years of hard work ahead of us before we can finish our education. I wish we were both going back to Ann Arbor tomorrow.

"Mamie, you know we must learn to face all kinds of situations to make us all-round workers for God. This experience of having to wait so many years before we can be together is just one of the spiritual gymnastics to develop the right kind of spiritual muscle and sinew."

"I suppose you're right again, David."

"At this time we are like the block of marble the sculptor finds and begins to shape by chipping off the rough corners. Every blow brings out more fully his ideal. So, Mamie, the rough stones in our lives may be those various trying experiences through which God allows us to pass. If we submit to them, they will serve as blows to bring out the figure of the Divine in us.

"I didn't mean to get serious," he said as he patted her arm. "Pardon me."

"That's a good lesson for me, David. I'll try to remember it when I step on a stone."

"It's time we were starting back," he said, taking her shawl. "We both have to be out early in the morning."

During those long years they met many times. When Mamie began to study medicine, they were together in school one full year in Ann Arbor. Then David left for New York to take his senior year in the Bellevue Medical College. Here he would get a wider experience in clinical medicine under the direction of the greatest medical authorities in this country.

Remembering the soul-winning objectives of his training, he took lodging in the mission home of Dr. George D. Dowkontt, a man of great faith who at that time was conducting a thriving medical missionary center in the slums of New York. David was given a small rear room with meager appointments. Concerning it I heard him tell later, "I soon discovered I had a lonesome feeling. Just then a man came along and invited me to go to the mission with him. He took me into some poverty-stricken homes where there was nothing to eat and no comforts in life—then on to the mission. He gave me a glimpse of the world's need.

"When I went back to my room it looked different to me. The wallpaper, which hung down from the ceiling in one corner, looked like a beautiful scroll such as you see on Christmas cards. The old furniture was transformed into sixteenth-century antiques, which come so high today. The room was the same as when I left it—but I had changed. I had a glimpse of a world I had never known before."

David spent what spare time he had at the mission. It was not long before Dr. Dowkontt announced to him that he was to lead the mission meeting the next Tuesday night. In speaking of that experience, he said, "I began to make excuses—said I couldn't do it—but the reply came, 'Tut, tut, mon, but you are to lead that meeting.' I did."

Many times I have heard Dr. Paulson tell of those New York experiences. They had their part in developing a sympathy and love for the unfortunate classes of earth that he hadn't formerly possessed.

He was invited to take charge of a Sunday school class of boys who seemed more interested in snatching candy from one another, pulling hair, and crawling under the seats, than in the gospel of Christ.

"But I breathed a prayer to God," David said, "that I might love the unlovely and make the gospel so interesting that the boys would forget their pranks.

"Instead of a fond mother's embrace and the tender sympathy that was bestowed upon us in our childhood, these children had the blows of a drunken father and the curses of an equally fallen mother. Talk to these children of love—it had no meaning—it would only be conveyed in one way, and that was to *love* them."

One boy Tim, who had been troubling the other classes, was brought to Dr. Paulson's class. "He tried my patience to the uttermost," said David, "and almost broke up the class, so I dismissed him. The next Sunday he didn't come, and that worried me. My heart yearned for that boy Tim. I had read the words, 'Those whom we push off may be the ones whom Christ is especially seeking to save.' So I hunted up Tim and told him that I loved him, asked him to forgive me, and to come back. I assured him we would get along all right. He came back and was soon a changed boy."

Eager to do more for the boys, Paulson asked for the mission room every Sunday afternoon to meet with them. In they came pell-mell, stumbling over chairs and one another—dirty, ragged youngsters, alive with vermin.

Continuing the story, David said, "I told them about a God of love, who, 'like as a father pitieth his children,' pitied them (Ps. 103:13). I thought they would pitch me out of the room. They had been kicked, cuffed, and mistreated by their fathers. Why should they listen to anything about a God in heaven who would treat them as their fathers did?

"The thought came to me that I myself must love those youngsters. It is easy to feel sorry for them, but to love a dirty, rough street urchin whose hair was full of vermin—how could I do it? I asked God to put His love into my heart for them, and He answered my prayer."

The language of love is universal. If you feel kindly toward a dog, he will wag his tail and give you a look of recognition. Dr. Paulson could tell these children there was a God in heaven who loved them just as he did, only infinitely more so.

For weeks and months he worked with those boys. Speaking of his farewell meeting with them he said:

"I will never forget the last meeting we had together when I was to leave the city. Some of those children, with tears in their eyes, said, 'Dr. Paulson, who will love us when you're gone?' One of the sweetest experiences of my life was when I knelt down with those boys in that parting meeting and committed them to the Father of the fatherless and to that Friend that sticketh closer than a brother. 'The entrance of thy words giveth light,' even to the street Arabs of New York City.

"At that moment I rededicated my life to God and asked Him never to permit me to be a loveless being. Medical missionaries are needed who have so much love for fallen humanity, implanted in their hearts by the Spirit of God, that the condition of the most loathsome and unlovely will move them to go about doing good even as did our blessed Master."

The many experiences that came to Dr. Paulson in life, especially those he allowed to be used of God to further him toward his goal—that of being a minister of the double gospel, health and soul winning—he had well cataloged in his mind. He had no trouble in recalling the right one to fit the individual he was dealing with at the time. He also cherished the instruction he received during his year at Bellevue Medical College.

His work with the children of New York's slums served to make him more loving and compassionate with all classes of sufferers. After much prayer he decided to accept the invitation to join the medical staff of the Battle Creek Sanitarium.

CHAPTER FIVE

Now Ready to Fulfill Vow

David Paulson entered the Battle Creek Sanitarium in the spring of 1894, a dignified, well-dressed man of twenty-six, wearing a full beard trimmed to a point at the chin, like most professional men of those days. He proudly carried with him a diploma from the Bellevue Medical College of New York, and was ready to begin his lifework as a physician.

A born leader with a strong personality, an inspirational speaker, a conscientious man, a well-trained doctor with a fund of knowledge at his command, he soon won the confidence of his patients.

There was one incident in those early days of medical practice that influenced his entire life. Here's the story as he once told it:

"The first year I had charge of nervous and mental diseases. One patient, a prominent physician from a neighboring State, had the habit of dropping into my office every day for a little chat. He seemed to enjoy it, and it gave me an opportunity to study his case more closely than otherwise. One day he asked, 'Doctor, how old are you?'

"Glancing up quickly, I replied, 'Me? why, I'm twenty-six.' Then he said, 'I never knew a young man so full of information. You have a marvelous future before you.' Naturally I felt a bit flattered. That same afternoon a humble sort of patient came in and told me that the big doctor, my patient, was sitting out on the lawn ripping me up the back to fifteen or more of my patients. I couldn't believe it. I thought I was helping that doctor, but he with his disturbed mind was gloating over my inexperience as a young physician. Since then, when anyone flatters me I think of that noted physician. That incident drove me to God. I have come to the conclusion that a self-sufficient person may at times seem to be moving the world, but it is the humble, praying person who moves heaven."

Once established in Battle Creek, David Paulson found that the entire sanitarium personnel had become aroused to their duty to the poor and unfortunate in the city. The institution had already started a medical mission in Chicago's slum district, which reflected its influence on the entire group of workers in the Battle Creek Sanitarium. The nurses in Battle Creek were visiting the sick poor and other cases of need in town.

They entered homes, took off their coats, rolled up their sleeves, and cleaned house for the sick and aged. They gave treatments, prepared tasty food, and in other ways made the sick comfortable, giving their time and loving service without thought of being reimbursed.

A rescue mission was opened to reach the denizens of the saloons in Battle Creek. Services were held in the county jail. These workers felt that their ministry lifted them to a higher plane spiritually as they reached down to help the unfortunates out of the gutter.

Dr. Paulson entered into this worthy ministry wholeheartedly. He organized classes for all types of workers, from the medical staff, the nurses, heads of departments, down to the humblest workers in the institution. They not only studied the Bible for counsel on one's responsibility to the poor, but sought also to find health principles approved of heaven. Personal religion, integrity, the importance of ordering one's life by the precepts laid down by God Himself in His Word, were considered.

"If we live by principle," said Dr. Paulson, "steering straight ahead, sometimes we shall suit other people and sometimes we shall not, but we shall always be sure of pleasing God."

I remember how eagerly the class hung onto his words. With pencil and notebook in hand they jotted down word for word all the main points of his lectures.

"Dr. Paulson says we must make serving God the most important task of our lives," remarked Mrs. Blank, head of the department in which I was working.

My reply was that it sounded like a hard task for young people who are thinking more about themselves and the present than about their influence.

"You're right," she said, "but I think it pays to please God first. I wouldn't miss for anything on earth what I'm getting out of these lectures."

I assured her I attended them as often as I was able.

"I shall never forget an illustration about a churn that he gave us the other day," she said.

"What was that?" I asked.

"Well, he said we were all like broken stones in a churn."

"I don't understand. I must have missed that."

"The idea was that we are hundreds of young people

from different families and different parts of the country thrown together here like one family, and our dispositions could easily clash all the time."

"What does the churn have to do with it?" I asked.

"Oh," she said, "when you put some broken pieces of stone with sharp, jagged edges into a churn, and churn, and churn them, what happens? They come out smooth and polished. Do you get the idea?"

"Oh, I get it now," I smiled. "If we submit to the process of polishing, we will be better for it."

"Dr. Paulson said that if we have a definite purpose in our hearts," she continued, "no matter where we may be found, or under what circumstances we may be placed, that purpose will remain steadfast with us. Our personal influence amounts to little when not measured by principle. Those who, like Daniel, purpose in their hearts to do right, will pass through fire and water rather than sacrifice that principle."

We are told that if we had God's principles of righteous living in our hearts, they would serve as a master key that would unlock life's most desperate problems. He advised us never to ask permission to carry out our principle. "Let those with whom you associate," he said, "take for granted that you are true to principle. They will never think to question, for instance, whether you are honest or not. If we serve God from principle, He will make even our enemies to be at peace with us."

Dr. Paulson never taught a class or gave a lecture without first asking God's presence to be with him. For notes he used just key words.

He always had a large audience. One day I said,

"David, why is it you always draw such a big crowd whenever you lecture?"

"Oh, do you remember that text in Luke 17:37?"

"Well, no, I don't recall it."

"It says, 'Wheresoever the body is, thither will the eagles be gathered together.' I simply try to give them food. People will flock to you if you have something to feed them."

Continuing his talk on guiding principles, he said, "Those who weave the magnificent tapestries produced in Oriental countries work under the goods and see only the rough threads beneath, but they have in mind a definite pattern of the beautiful figure that is being wrought on top. Often in our daily work, seeing only the loose threads, we seem to have abundant reason for discouragement. If we work from principle, we may be sure that a divine hand has worked out for us a glorious pattern that will abide through all eternity."

Whenever Dr. Paulson gave us a good principle there would always come with it an illustration to fix it in the memory of his listeners. Here's another one: "An eaves trough made of ordinary lumber may carry off as much water, provided it is so hung as to catch the drops, as one made of silver. So, although from a human standpoint we may not seem to be very promising, if we are willing to be placed of God where the droppings of His blessing can fall upon us, we shall be happy ourselves and a blessing and help to others."

"I learned," he said, "as a personal experience that if a man bows before his Creator, he never needs to bow before his fellow men. The Lord will see to it that he has standing room."

Dr. Paulson's greatest delight seemed to be in inculcating principles of truth on the hearts and minds of the young and old, if they had a heart to listen and absorb. He awakened in his students a desire to delve deeper into the science of the healing art, as well as into the art of healing the soul.

"If we have sown the genuine gospel seed in tears," he said, "in the day of judgment we shall find that not so much of it has been wasted as we may have imagined. The gospel seed is immortal, and like money, may pass through the hands of many before it actually comes to the one whom God intends it shall reach. God says definitely, 'My word shall not return unto me void.' That which from a human standpoint may seem like a dismal failure, when viewed from God's wisdom may prove to be a signal triumph."

As a physician in the Battle Creek Sanitarium he soon found a large audience among the workers and patients, who were eager to sit at his feet and learn of the gospel of health and salvation. Not long after he began those classes he realized that they gave him courage to carry out his lifework and keep his vow to God.

CHAPTER SIX

A Diamond Mine and a Dark Basement

David Paulson, during those years of study in Battle Creek College and the University of Michigan, became a close friend of Dr. John Harvey Kellogg, medical director of the Battle Creek Sanitarium.

Dr. Kellogg was a remarkable man, short in stature, with dark hair, piercing eyes, and pleasingly round face. He always wore a goatee, which in those days gave him a professional appearance. He had a keen intellect and the executive ability to put his unique ideas into action.

Dr. Kellogg had been in charge of the Battle Creek Sanitarium for many years and had brought it to the eminent success it enjoyed. He was famous as a distinguished surgeon, author of many books, promoter of healthful living, and orginator of health foods.

In those days he did much toward giving needed counsel, direction, and even financial assistance to David Paulson and other young men who were struggling to get ahead.

Dr. Kellogg became deeply interested in opening a medical mission in Chicago for the poorest, most needy classes. He felt such an urge to do it that it was on his mind continually. He talked and prayed often with others about it.

One day as Dr. Kellogg was sitting alone at his desk, a humble-looking man was ushered in. Looking up, the doctor recognized him as a guest in the sanitarium and at once saw that the man was perturbed—his face showed deep concern.

Once seated, the visitor said, "Dr. Kellogg, I don't know why, but there is something that has been on my mind for weeks. I can't get away from it."

"Well, man, do tell me what it is."

"You'll be as surprised as I have been all these weeks when you hear my story."

"Do tell me, sir."

"Well, bluntly, it's just this—I want to know, Doctor, if I should give you a sum of money, what would you do with it?"

"Do!" The doctor's face radiated his delight as he rose from his chair and began to pace the room. "What would I do with a sum of money? Why, man, we've been praying for weeks for money! We want to go down to Chicago and open a medical mission for the neglected peoples of that city."

"That's just what I want," said the man.

"Why, you're answering our prayers, my brother. Nothing could please me more."

The visitor then identified himself as John Wessels, one of the Wessels brothers who owned a large diamond mine in South Africa. He handed Dr. Kellogg a check for forty thousand dollars to start a medical mission in Chicago. The good news leaped like wildfire to David Paulson and the other students in Ann Arbor, all of whom were deeply interested in the new project for Chicago's needy poor.

The medical mission in Chicago had a humble beginning. In the early spring of 1893 Dr. Kellogg made a personal trip to Chicago to find the most neglected, neediest part of the city. He was advised to go to the old Harrison Street police station near Van Buren Street. As he strode quickly to the sergeant's desk, he said, "Officer, I'm Dr. Kellogg of the Battle Creek Sanitarium."

"Oh, yes, sir," the sergeant said as he rose to greet the doctor. "What can I do for you?"

"Will you kindly tell me where I can find the dirtiest, wickedest, neediest spot in all Chicago?"

The desk sergeant looked at him in amazement as he replied. "You're on the right spot, Doctor. Anywhere within two blocks of this station you'll find just what you're looking for."

"That's exactly what I want, officer. Thank you."

Days were consumed as Dr. Kellogg searched high and low, here and there, near and far, for a room large enough for a clinic and a bathhouse. It was the year of the first World's Fair in Chicago in 1893. Every available place has been taken by saloonkeepers, restaurateurs, and gamblers, who expected to get rich quick from the World's Fair. Many places had been looked at, but they were all either too large, too small, or too high priced.

Dr. Kellogg had prayed earnestly that the Lord would guide him to the right spot, but now he was at his wit's end. He and his secretary stood one day on the curb looking down into the gutter on Van Buren Street. Dr. Kellogg, in telling that story later, said, "That moment seemed the darkest in our whole experience. Forty thousand dollars had been contributed for that work, but we could find no place in which to start." Little did they know that the spot on which they stood was but a few rods from the place the mission would be established.

Just across the street was the Pacific Garden Mission, where Dr. Kellogg had called first in his search for a location. Col. George R. Clarke, the leader of the mission, had extended to him an invitation to locate near the mission so the two institutions could work together. But now Colonel Clarke had passed away, and there seemed to be no opening in that direction.

"It's near traintime," said Dr. Kellogg to his secretary. In telling the story later he said, "We started for the depot, downhearted, but still not discouraged, expecting to go home for the fifth time without deciding on a place to locate."

Glancing once more across the street, his secretary said, "Look, look, Dr. Kellogg! Do you see what I see? That sign in the window?"

"What sign?"

"The one right there in the Pacific Garden Mission. It says, 'Rooms to Rent.' "

"Upon my word! There was no sign when I looked the last time. Now there it is. Come on, let's hurry over. There's no time to lose."

They met Harry Monroe, the new leader of the mission. He was cordial and seemed interested in the prospect of having Dr. Kellogg and his associates cooperate with the mission work. Dr. Kellogg was astounded as he was led to the dirty old basement, almost entirely underground, at Customhouse Place around the corner from the Pacific Garden Mission.

The first job was to thoroughly clean and paint the entire basement. Then a corner was partitioned off for a clinic. Equipment for baths, laundry, and fumigation was installed in the large room.

When the rooms were ready, in came the men, thirty or forty a day, not only covered with filth and vermin on the outside of their bodies, but with minds debased with liquor and narcotics. All needed their clothes washed and fumigated. Clean clothing was provided for those who needed it badly, and there were many, many in that class. There was also a cookstove and a large soup kettle. Every night the latter was full of steaming-hot delicious soup for the mission. After the services the men crowded forward—four hundred or more—to get the hot bean soup and zwieback, for which they were glad to pay only a penny a bowl. No one was turned away hungry. No wonder one of the men said to a comrade, "Come on in, Jack; here's where you get soup, soap, and salvation."

This little bathhouse was like the inn on the Jericho road in Bible times, only here were hundreds of men, instead of one as in the Bible story, who had fallen among thieves. Many of them had had their hearts as well as their heads broken.

This medical mission that Dr. Kellogg was instrumental in starting, with the help of the forty thousand dollars, was now in full operation. Dr. Howard Rand, Dr. Daniel H. Kress, and Dr. E. R. Caro, all schoolmates of Dr. Paulson in Ann Arbor, affiliated with this Chicago Medical Mission for a time after their graduation. They patched the broken heads and limbs and asked God to heal the broken hearts.

Ofttimes these doctors were asked to report on the progress of their work. I remember one story from Dr. Rand. He said:

"One bitter cold morning when the bathhouse was full of crooks—the most wicked and dangerous in all Chicago—there appeared a big, strapping Irish policeman at the door in full uniform, with his club in hand.

" 'Mornin', Doc,' he said, with a broad grin on his face.

" 'Good morning, officer, won't you come in?'

" 'Don't mind if I do. Shure and what are all thim bums doin' here?' he asked.

" 'Why officer, this is a dispensary and bathhouse. We give these fellows a chance to clean up, and we look after them medically.'

" 'Shure and that's grand, but how much dough do they hav' to give yez?'

" 'Dough!' I said with a smile. 'We never see any. This service is all free to the men.'

" 'Free to thim bums?'

" 'Yes, we doctors are giving our time to help them.'

" 'The saints preserve yez! Why, thim guys are the worst in all Chicago, and there's enough of 'em in here to blow this whole place to smithereens.'

" 'Yes, we know it,' the doctor smiled, 'but they're in distress and need help. The Good Book doesn't say, When your well-respected, influential brother falls into the ditch, you're to help him out. No, it just says, 'Your brother' and we are all brothers.'

" 'Shure, and you're right there. I brought me shillelagh wid me—thought I'd be after needin' it. But look—so many in here there's just room for thim to stand, and as peaceful as lambs! Glory be! I never thought that me eyes would be lookin' at anything like this.'

" 'You're quite right, officer,' I replied, patting him on the shoulder. 'I suppose you notice there's no profanity, no hard language, and no jostling in here. I think we have about sixty men here this morning, and the room is supposed to accommodate only twelve.'

" 'Shure, and I'm after thinkin' they's a couple o' hundred waiting outside.'

" 'Is that so?' I inquired. 'It's a bitter cold morning for them to stand in line very long.'

" 'Shure, Doc, and I'm telling yez if thim tough guys were together anywheres else on the street it would take a half dozen of us police to keep 'em straight.'

" 'Were they orderly when you came in?'

" 'Oh, shure, they were standing two and two way down the street and 'round the corner. Didn't yez send a man out to line 'em up?'

" 'No, officer, they did that themselves.'

" 'Well, I niver—they's all different—you know.'

" 'You mean they are different nationalities.'

" 'Yes—then there's alley rats an' barflies.'

" 'Pray tell me, officer, what are barflies?'

" 'Ha! yez don't know our way of talkin' down here. A barfly goes from bar to bar moochin' a nip from other men at the bar. Most of 'em are stewed. Good thing it's warm in here, and clean, too,' he said, as he glanced around. 'Brick walls an' bare floors—that's all right. No need for any of that gingerbread stuff down here.'

" 'You're right, officer, we have plenty of good clean clothing for them, though.'

" 'Oh, shure, Doc. Come to think about it, I didn't see any gloves or mittens on the guys out there on the street.'

" 'Possibly there were not many of them with shirts, either.'

" 'Faith, and the poor coots—no shirts? I did see one old fellow with rags tied around his neck and on his wrists and ankles. I wonder if he's tryin to fool hisself into thinkin' he had a shirt on?'

" 'We find many men like that. You know they keep out a lot of the wind that way.'

" 'That's the idee.'

" 'Officer, what I would like to know is, How did you happen to observe those men so closely? I thought you police were usually tough and hard with this class of citizens.'

" 'You're shure grand, Doc, I'll tell yez. It's made me all trembly inside to see thim toughs perk up at a little kindness. Praise be to yez.' "

Many of those men who had reached the bottom of degradation came back the long road to respectability and usefulness through the instruction they received at the mission and the example of Christianity at work at the dispensary. One of those men who stood in line on the street the day of the policeman's visit, raised his hand for prayer at the mission that same night. As he did so, his ragged sleeve fell down, leaving his bare arm reaching heavenward. He didn't reach in vain. He became a successful rescue mission evangelist—Tom Mackey, of whom you'll learn later.

On certain days the dispensary was open to women and children only. Louise Burkhardt, a nurse, was always there on those days. Women with their sick children came in droves and filled the place.

My sister, then a senior medical student in Northwestern University, had office hours in the clinic of this basement dispensary. One day Dr. Paulson called on her—I say, one day—the days when he called were becoming more and more frequent as the time was drawing near when she would graduate, June, 1896. Then they would be ready for the most important step in their lives—their wedding day.

"Of course you know, David, about our new venture down here in the slums."

"Oh, yes. You refer to that old building next door."

"That's it. I'm probably not telling you any news about it. You know it once was an old church, and had long since been used as a cheap lodging house."

"Yes, Mamie, I know."

"Well, dirt and filth of every kind had been accumulating for years. It was so thick that it kept several men busy for many days carting off the rubbish."

"I heard that dirt was piled up nearly to the tops of the windows."

"That's right. It was terrible. I saw them carting it off."

"I believe it's to be used as a workingmen's home."

"That's right again. You seem to have the whole story, but it had become a hiding place for criminals. They were all driven out. Of course there was danger of trouble with such characters, but the Lord protected all of us, and that was sufficient. One of the first to be converted was the manager, and many of the men from there are also clean Christian men today."

American Medical Missionary College, 1895-1910.

"Yes, a lot of good has been done since that building was opened."

Thus a second building was acquired for the use of the Chicago Medical Mission.

An organization called the International Medical Missionary and Benevolent Association was formed. Under this the various medical missionary enterprises operated. This became a nationwide organization, as medical and rescue missions, jail evangelism, State prison visitations, and some institutions for the care of children and wayward girls spread throughout the country.

In Chicago one institution after another opened, so that all classes of need were reached. The initial forty thousand dollars donated was used to purchase a large building on the south side of Chicago, 28 33d Place, which was equipped for a sanitarium. The earnings from this institution were used in support of the various charities.

In September, 1895, a medical school was founded, called the American Medical Missionary College. This school was unique in that it was the only one in the country that included in its curriculum a thorough course in Bible and missionary methods besides all the subjects required of an accredited medical college. Its graduates were prepared to serve as medical missionaries in home and foreign lands.

Dr. Paulson was all for this school; in fact, he and Dr. Kellogg spent many hours talking and praying about the enterprise. When Dr. Kellogg first came to Dr. Paulson and said, "Paulson, what would you think of starting a medical missionary college here in Battle Creek and in Chicago?" Dr. Paulson looked eagerly at

Dr. Kellogg and said, "What would I think? Why, of course, that's just the thing to do. At the moment I can think of a dozen reasons why we should do it."

"What are some of your reasons, Paulson?"

"Well, I received an excellent training in medicine while I was studying in Ann Arbor and Bellevue Medical College, New York, but never once did I get a word of instruction on how to heal the soul as well as the body. You know, Dr. Kellogg, there are a lot of people who are sick physically because they are sick spiritually. How are we going to train young people to go all over the world as medical missionaries without giving instruction in missionary methods as well as in medicine?"

"That's fine, Paulson. I see we are both thinking along the same line. Patients in a state of fear and despondency must be helped out of that condition before we can expect to heal them physically."

"How right you are, Dr. Kellogg."

Dr. Paulson headed the departments of instruction in nervous, mental, and skin diseases in the American Medical Missionary College, and held that position throughout the life of the school. Some of his classmates in Ann Arbor were members of the faculty. Among them were Dr. W. A. George, professor of chemistry, Drs. D. H. and Lauretta Kress, Drs. John Byington, W. B. Holden, Howard Rand, Alfred Olsen, E. R. Caro, and others. The school operated jointly in Battle Creek and in Chicago. The first class of about one hundred students was accommodated easily in the Battle Creek Sanitarium and its many cottages. In Chicago a large four-story brick building was leased to house the class and its activities. This building had two wings at the rear, facing the alley, or rather the elevated lines, where trains rumbled noisily past at all hours of the day and night—right in the midst of Chicago's crime belt.

A sign across the building under the upper windows read, MEDICAL MISSIONARY COLLEGE, and below under the next row of windows was another—MEDICAL MISSIONARY TRAINING SCHOOL FOR NURSES.

In this building the students slept, ate, attended classes, assisted in the clinics, minor surgery, and maternity. In one wing shut off by itself was the dissecting room.

Crime and drunkenness were all about them. The women students were always accompanied by an escort when making a call at night.

The spiritual and inspirational training eclipsed the miserable conditions of crime, squalor, and filth surrounding the students.

Years later I was talking with one of the nurses about the old days, when 1926 Wabash Avenue was mentioned. This nurse affectionately said, "Dear old 1926! I never think of the filth and the drunken men who were all about us down there, but I always remember the food I got for my soul." Then she told me about the soul-stirring classes she had attended and how her life was changed.

There's where, four years later, Dr. and Mrs. Paulson found a great field for their chosen work.

The theoretical instruction in the medical school was given largely in Battle Creek by members of the sanitarium faculty. In addition to the sanitarium physicians, who also taught subjects in Chicago, there were eminent specialists in Chicago from the Cook County and other leading hospitals, who conducted clinics.

Many of the graduates from this medical school won honorable degrees in London, Edinburgh, and Dublin, preparatory to entering foreign fields. It closed its doors in 1910, when the College of Medical Evangelists was established at Loma Linda, California.

The undergraduates in the American Medical Missionary College were accepted by the Northwestern Medical School, where they completed their course. A dozen or more graduates of the American Medical Missionary College became not only teachers in the College of Medical Evangelists but also cofounders and promoters largely responsible for the growth of the school, some continuing with the College of Medical Evangelists until their death. Today the living members of the 191 graduates of American Medical Missionary College are among the alumni of the College of Medical Evangelists in Los Angeles.

Some of those who became pillars of strength in the College of Medical Evangelists are Drs. Julia White, Edward Risley, A. Q. Shryock, Florence Keller, Lyra Hunt George, D. D. Comstock, Benton Colver, August Larson, and others.

During all these years Dr. Paulson never forgot his vow to God to give his life helping humanity both physically and spiritually. In Chicago there seemed a wider field for such endeavor than in the Battle Creek Sanitarium. Occasionally the thought would flash through his mind, "Does the Lord want me to go to Chicago?"

CHAPTER SEVEN

Stepping Out by Faith

In 1896 my sister graduated with high honors from the medical school of Northwestern University in Evanston, Illinois. Eagerly David Paulson had waited for this event, because it meant the consummation of their hopes—their wedding.

She began her medical practice in the Battle Creek Sanitarium, and soon became a specialist in gynecology. Both were unusually busy during that summer, each carrying a list of from fifty to eighty patients a day.

They had planned a quiet home wedding for December. Then they would take the first train after the wedding for New York, where they could both take postgraduate work while on their honeymoon.

The entire sanitarium group had a different idea. They had no intention of letting their two doctors get married and slip away from them so quietly. There was growing excitement—something had to be done. Dr. Kellogg, medical director, took charge of the situation by sending out a general invitation to a social evening in the gymnasium.

In a few hours the gymnasium was transformed—all the gymnasium equipment was pushed back against the wall, a platform appeared covered with carpeting, long runners were laid down the center aisle, and the large room was filled with chairs to the doors. When the palms, shrubbery, and flowering plants arrived from the sanitarium greenhouse the gymnasium took on a festive air.

Upstairs in the bride's chamber a nervous young woman doctor was getting dressed in her soft-blue traveling suit to become the bride of her beloved David. The large gymnasium filled to the doors, and outside the crowds extended down the corridor and out the main entrance of the building. Did the entire west end of the city come to see Dr. Paulson married? was in the thoughts of many. The chaplain, L. McCoy, performed the ceremony and the nervous David and Mamie said, "I do."

It was long past midnight before the train for New York pulled in at the station. When the wedding party arrived at the depot, the medical students were waiting with their pockets full of rice. It was a great send-off for two surprised young doctors.

Regardless of the joy of honeymooning, they didn't forget their future work. The three weeks were profitably spent in postgraduate study. Before leaving the metropolis they visited relatives in Pleasantville, New York, and were shown through the famous Sing Sing Prison a few miles away. Their guide, one of the officers of the prison, decided to play a practical joke. When they came to the dark dungeon the guide suggested they step inside. They no sooner had done so than they found themselves locked in and the lights turned off.

"O David! I'm frightened," Mamie cried.

"Don't worry; we have each other, my dear." Soon the lights came on, and they saw a broad grin on the face of the guard, who had spotted them as newlyweds.

"I pity the poor culprits who land in there."

"You're right, lady," said the officer. "Too bad they can't learn before they reach this place."

After their return to Battle Creek, Mamie gradually lost her childhood name and became known far and near as Dr. Mary.

Dr. Paulson's duties as teacher in the medical school took him to Chicago on regular days each week. Thus he was in close touch with the work there. Any calls for help or for workers met a ready response from David.

About this time W. S. Sadler, a promising young man, was sent to Chicago to help with the administration of the Chicago Medical Mission. Later Mr. Sadler graduated from the American Medical Missionary College and became known as the author of several books on psychology and the relation of the mind to the body. One of his best-known books is *Mind at Mischief, Tricks and Deceptions of the Conscience, and How to Cope With it.*

In 1898 Dr. Kellogg launched a magazine called *The Life Boat,* in the interest of the Chicago Medical Mission. W. S. Sadler became the first editor. All over the country contributors to the mission read in *The Life Boat* thrilling accounts of the work.

The good work in Chicago grew rapidly. There were about a dozen centers of activity in the city, under the direction of the Chicago Medical Mission. The Workingmen's Home provided a large rugmaking industry, and at one time kept two thousand men at work cleaning Chicago's streets at no expense to the city.

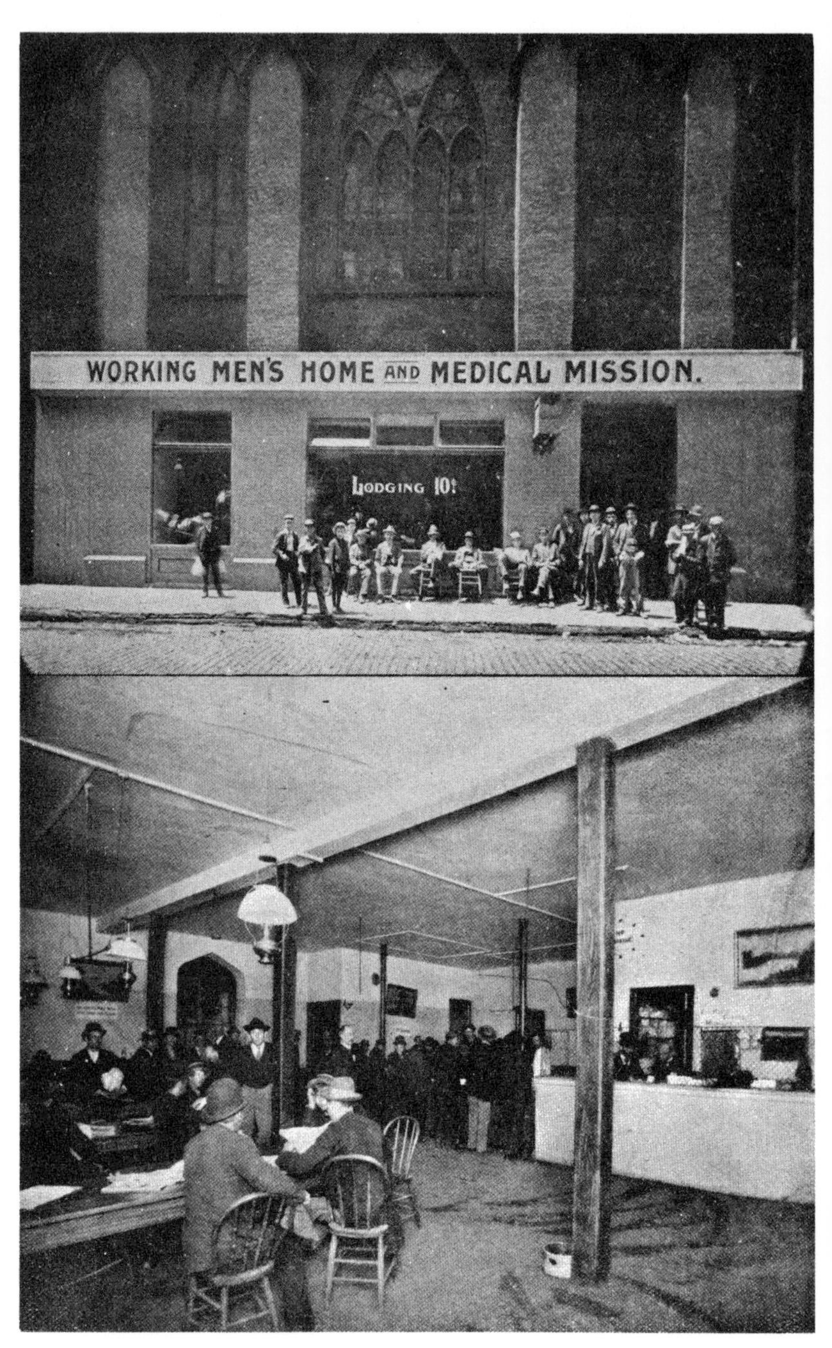

Top: Headquarters of the Chicago Medical Mission, 1893.
Bottom: Office and reading room, Workingmen's Home.

When Dr. Kellogg left for an extended absence in Europe, Dr. Paulson was made acting director of the sanitarium. The heavy program, weighty problems, and long hours began to take their toll. It was thought that if he had a residence a few miles out from the city, he would have more hours of quiet and rest. A lake villa was prepared for the Paulsons about four miles away on the shores of Lake Goguac. When they were ready to enjoy it, W. S. Sadler arrived from Chicago. That was in the late spring of 1899.

When Mr. Sadler was ushered into Dr. Paulson's office he said, "Dr. Paulson, I came up here to see if I could get some young people to help me in Chicago."

"Well, Sadler, you came to the right place. What's the problem?"

"Doctor, you know our work is gradually branching out to take in more and more classes of people who need help."

"Good, Sadler, go on."

"What we need now is young people to visit in the homes of the poor and render any service necessary."

"I can see, Sadler, there's a large field that we have not at all covered. I'll call the board together and we'll talk it over."

Mr. Sadler stated his needs to the board, and then said, "What I want is some members of the freshman class of nurses who have been in training but a few weeks."

At once the expression on the face of every member of the board showed opposition.

"We can't see any light in such a move," one member said.

Another asked, "Have you given this proposition any serious thought?"

"Oh, yes, indeed I have."

"Well, I don't see how you could advise it when you think of these young folks from sheltered homes and from the farms, being sent out to work without training in the slums of such a large city as Chicago."

"I think it will do them good to get in direct contact with the needs of humanity," Dr. Paulson said.

"Of course," said Mr. Sadler, "we have no intention of turning young people out without proper supervision."

The discussion continued until minutes dragged into hours. Finally another member of the board spoke up: "Dr. Paulson is worn out. He needs a vacation. Suppose we arrange to let both Drs. David and Mary Paulson go to Chicago with a group of these young people?"

Dr. Paulson in telling the story said: "Mrs. Paulson and I left our little cottage at Lake Goguac the next day. We took with us forty of the freshman class of nurses who had volunteered to go to Chicago and give their time to work for the most needy people there. They had to find work to pay for all their expenses except their room rent."

All the students were nicely accommodated in the large building at 1926 Wabash Avenue, as well as both the Drs. Paulson.

Dr. Paulson said he had called these students together before they left Battle Creek and had told them they had to support themselves in Chicago. Only those were accepted who felt a call from God. The class was willing to do anything to earn their board and other expenses, to get any experience in working for the unfortunates. They had had only a few weeks' training as nurses, but Mrs. Emma L. Allison, of wide experience among the poor in the Bohemian district of Chicago, came with the class of forty young people from Battle Creek.

Not only had Mrs. Allison years of experience as a worker for the poor in Chicago, but she also was in charge of a home for homeless men and boys in Battle Creek, and had worked for many years conducting a Christian home for men and boys in Ann Arbor.

Her early life was tragic. During a storm at sea she had been prematurely born two hours before the ship sank. She had been strapped to a nurse, and later picked up by a vessel bound for New York. She was six months old when found by her parents, who had been rescued and taken to England.

When twenty years old she was supposed to have died of typhoid fever. The funeral services were being held when her father, stooping to kiss her goodby, noticed the muscles of her face twitching. Restoratives administered immediately revived her. Later, when she was a mother of several children, they were captured by the Indians and their house burned. Such was the experience of the woman selected to mother the forty students who came to Chicago with Dr. Paulson, She was loved by all.

Dr. Paulson continued his story, "I told the students to spend a day praying about getting work. The next day we called them together, and there were fifteen of those girls who said they would like to nurse. Then

I said, 'Now we will have to pray for fifteen jobs.' "

During the next thirty-six hours exactly fifteen requests came in over the telephone for practical nurses —trained nurses were not wanted. For instance, an old woman who had broken her leg needed an attendant while her son was working. Others were past the critical stage of some severe illness. For such, a helper was needed rather than a trained nurse.

"I placed those girls out, and they earned enough so they could have taken care of all of us. Our prayers were answered. It seemed to me it was a divine certificate that we were on the right track and that it pays to launch out into the deep."

The class was asked to seek God for wisdom to lead them into various channels of missionary work. There were the Life Boat Mission, cottage meetings, care of the sick and needy in their homes, the selling of the *Life Boat* magazine, gospel work in the jails, and work in the various dispensaries, wherever they would be able to do and receive the most good. As they acquired an experience in one line, they were transferred to another line, to get an all-round training while there.

Dr. Paulson wrote: "An hour was spent each morning on instruction in methods of work. Tears of joy trickled down the cheeks of these young workers and an intense longing was born in their hearts to give the gospel to even the least of Chicago's unfortunates. Scarcely a word of criticism or faultfinding was heard among this class of forty young people who came from Battle Creek with Mrs. Paulson and me. The great thought uppermost in every mind was, How can I best improve my Heaven-sent opportunities?"

Every one of those students had to decide personally whether to follow God's leading even though he couldn't see ahead, or follow other lines that appeared more attractive.

Dr. Paulson had a little story he often told to young people who were undecided which path to take—the one that offered many attractions or the one that looked uncertain and misty ahead. He said:

"When Joseph went down to Egypt there were no great attractions for him. When Daniel took the first steps toward becoming prime minister, the lions' den was on the road. He had a timetable, too, I think. When you see a great providence painted on the sky, the devil paints it there, God's providences are always veiled. We accept them by faith. God says, 'Strait is the gate, and narrow is the way, which leadeth unto life.' As you go you begin to see the beautiful picture the Lord paints for you. The devil says, 'I will give you the world,' but the cross is on Christ's road."

Today those forty young people are veteran medical missionaries with long years of service in this and foreign lands. Their training in the slums of Chicago prepared them for service in Africa, China, and other far-off neglected lands at that time shrouded in darkness, superstition, and ignorance.

Dr. David Paulson turned his back on the prospects of leadership in a large and prosperous sanitarium, and, from a human standpoint, buried himself and his talents in the heart of Chicago. He lived with the students at "1926," the old brick watch factory, which before that had been a home for the friendless.

A noonday prayer meeting at the old Chicago Mission.

CHAPTER EIGHT

"I'm a Stenographer, Sir"

Dr. Paulson's responsibilities at the Chicago Medical Mission had grown in a few weeks to a point where a full-time stenographer was needed. There was no money available for salaries—the workers were all donating their time. He felt that help should come either from one of the workers seeking experience or from someone who had received charity.

One day he said to Mr. Sadler, his co-worker, "Suppose we ask the Lord to send us a stenographer."

"That's a good idea. Shall we pray now?"

The two men knelt in prayer in Dr. Paulson's office, and continued to make it their business to pray together every day. About two days later a square-jawed, pale-faced, shabby-looking English fellow edged his way into Dr. Paulson's office and in a low, hesitant voice asked, "Are you Dr. Paulson?"

"Yes, man, I am. Come in."

"I'm wondering, would you do something for a poor fellow?"

"Why, yes, what do you mean?"

"I mean, sir, I have no work. I want a job."

"Well, my man, what can you do?"

"I'm a stenographer, sir."

In telling about it Dr. Paulson said:

"When that fellow shambled into my office in ragged clothes—a typical bum—it was hard for me to think the Lord had sent an answer to my prayer done up in that kind of package. I didn't know what to say, but after hesitating, I replied, 'I've been praying for a stenographer.'

" 'Well sir,' he said, 'I've been praying for a job.'

"Without stopping to think, I said, 'I think you and I ought to thank the Lord we met.'

"With tears of gratitude he said, 'Thank you, sir.'

"We knelt down on our knees, and I thanked the Lord that this young fellow, who said he could do stenographic work, had come. He thanked the Lord he had found a job. I called Mr. Sadler in to try him out. Mr. Sadler eyed me, suspecting a joke was being played on him. Then he looked the man up and down suspiciously and took him downstairs. By-and-by he came back smiling, and said, 'If that fellow can write out what I have given him, he's a genius.'

"Pretty soon he returned again, 'Upon my word, here it is just as I gave it, word for word. You sure have gotten yourself a good man. He's a wonder.'

" 'Sadler, you know we prayed for a stenographer. You didn't expect the Lord to send a second-rate or a third-rate stenographer when he answered our prayers, did you?'

" 'Well, that's so.'

" 'Remember, Sadler, the main thing in a stenographer is to take dictation and transcribe it—it's not a question of being on dress parade.'

"He was a queer freak—he would get stubborn sometimes. One time I remember he didn't want to take down my talk, so he sat back there during the address and never wrote a word. I went to him afterward and said, 'Say, man, why didn't you take that down?'

" 'If you want that, I can write it out.'

" 'What! You mean you can write out my whole speech without any notes?'

" 'Oh, yes, I can do it.'

" 'Then I wish you would.

" 'All right, I will.'

"A miracle happened. The next morning he handed me fourteen pages of typewritten matter, and for the life of me, I could scarcely tell but that it was verbatim.

"He had an amazing memory, and knew the king's English backward and forward, yet he didn't have sense to do other things that a child could do—not even lace his shoes. No wonder he dropped into the dispensary occasionally to get some rags to tie around his shoes to hold them on his feet.

"He was with us a couple of years, and was a perfect godsend, happy to work for his board and room and a dollar a week for spending money."

The mission clothed him, so he looked as well dressed as anyone, after he learned to use shoelaces. He also learned many things not found in a book.

The last news we had from him was that as a well-dressed, well-informed, upstanding lecturer he was traveling through the South on a lecture tour. Just one of the many ships adrift on the sea of life that found a safe harbor.

Group of converts of a Chicago rescue mission, 1898.

CHAPTER NINE

Gems From Chicago's Gutters

Tom Mackey became one of the brightest gems ever picked from the slime and scum of Chicago's cesspool of crime. A stocky man, with black curly hair, he had a quick temper and was always ready for a fight. It was in 1894, in the old days of the basement dispensary, that the mission found him.

I heard him say one day, "On the very day I was converted God stayed my hand from committing an awful crime." He referred to having beaten a man nearly to death on the street in front of the Pacific Garden Mission.

He said, "That night at the mission I heard a man say that he had been kept from a life like mine for fifteen years. So I raised my hand. I heard one of the fellows back of me say, 'Curly is going to play the religious dodge.' Bless God, I have been playing it ever since. I started on a missionary tour that night, and I've never reached the end of it.

"When I came to God I was such a crooked guy that no one would trust me. Detectives used to be on my track, but now I have other detectives—goodness and mercy—they follow me all the days of my life."

Dr. Paulson improved every opportunity to encourage Tom Mackey in his new life. When Tom returned from a nine months' gospel campaign in Minneapolis, he found his way up to Battle Creek to Dr. Paulson's office.

"Doctor, the other day on the train, as I was returning from Minneapolis, I went over in my mind the old days, when the Chicago Medical Mission was started. I can see today the faces of those sympathetic nurses and doctors who were constantly called upon to battle every form of sin and disease."

"You were in the midst of those experiences, weren't you, Mackey?"

"Yes, I surely was. I can see even now the old fumigator, where the men would clean their clothing and do their washing in the free laundry. The men would stand around wrapped in sheets or blankets while their clothing was being fumigated."

"Did Dr. Kellogg visit the dispensary often in those days?"

"Yes, Dr. Paulson, he did, and I'm glad he did. I can see him today kneeling in prayer by the side of one of those poor sinners who was wrapped in a sheet. I can remember the lunch counter that was established in the hard winter of 1893-94, after the World's Fair. There were thousands of hungry women and children, and hundreds of men were driven almost to madness by the suffering of their families. At that lunch counter these people could buy a big bowl of soup and some liberal slices of zwieback for a penny."

"I missed the inspiration of that first year at the dispensary. You know, Mackey, I was in New York."

"Well, it was at this time, Dr. Paulson, that I came in contact with the dispensary. I was one of those men."

"Tell me about it, Mackey."

"All right, I will. I had had nothing to eat for several days. I was hungry and penniless, but had no desire to steal, for I had been converted in the mission.

"Fortunately for me, Dr. Kellogg was present on this particular day and learned of my need. He paid for a bowl of soup for me, brought it to me himself, and spoke very kindly to me. He even called me brother. That somehow touched my heart in a peculiar way. I knew there was nothing in the world that could make a man like him and a man like me brothers. I was ignorant, friendless, penniless, while he was an eminent physician, a noted educator, and a man of God. I didn't understand how it could all be, but he made me feel that it was so, and I was glad it was. The bowl of soup was a turning point in my career. I believe it saved my life."

"Your experience, Mackey, is a striking example of the power of God to save a sinner."

"I should say it is. Well, Dr. Kellogg asked me to give my testimony for the benefit of the four hundred down-and-outers who were at the lunch counter. That was my first effort to talk to sinners. It was a hard thing for me to do, but I stood up and said something. I don't remember a word I said, but I must have told about my conversion. I have been telling the story of salvation ever since."

Tom Mackey spent the remainder of his life as a successful mission evangelist, traveling over the Midwest States and on the West Coast.

There was Dick Lane, a professional thief, an expert at it, known throughout the country as a notorious safecracker, who had served time in seven different penitentiaries.

One dark night the authorities were searching for him—where should he go and what should he do? He saw a tiny light in the Pacific Garden Mission on Van Buren Street.

Years later Harry Monroe, leader of the mission, told the story of Dick Lane's conversion.

"One night a tall, dignified, well-dressed stranger stalked into the mission, down the aisle, and took a seat near the front. He listened intently to the service, sitting in silence all through the meeting. Occasionally he brushed a tear from his eyes. When at the close of the sermon an appeal was made, his hand was first to go up, asking for prayers. I never had seen him before and hardly knew what it meant for a stranger of his appearance to come forward in a rescue mission in such an earnest way. I asked what his purpose was for the future. He said, 'I'm going to live a clean life.' "

Dr. Paulson told us that Dick Lane had begun stealing as early as he could remember—stole from his mother on her deathbed. He even stole while in prison. One day while Lane was working in the kitchen a farmer came to sell chickens. Dick wiggled one out of sight and into the oven. One of the prisoners who saw him do it told the warden. The farmer insisted that he had brought twelve chickens, but there were only eleven accounted for. Dick, fearing detection, slipped the chicken out of the oven and into the ash can. By the time the warden began a search for the chicken, it wasn't to be found. The warden asked, "What did you do with that chicken, Dick?"

His apparently innocent reply was, "You wouldn't think that of *me* would you?" So the other prisoner got a reprimand for accusing him.

After Dick Lane's conversion he was a great help in the mission, where he would come often to tell others what the Lord had done for him. He had been living on stolen money, and had spent, on an average, sixty-five dollars a day. After his conversion he got a job cleaning windows in the *Record-Herald* building at one dollar a day. Before his death he had risen from window washer to manager of a department on the *Record-Herald* and had bought and paid for a comfortable home in the suburbs.

Can the Lord save crooks? Certainly. Dick Lane said that in the old life there were plenty of times he wanted to be honest, but when he saw money he could not resist taking it. After his conversion he had opportunity to steal thousands of dollars, but he was faithful to the Bible injunction, "Let him that stole steal no more."

There was another gem from the gutter who enlisted Dr. Paulson's interest in a special way. Samuel Coombs had been with Lord Wolseley in his famous British military expedition into Egypt. While in the army he acquired the drink habit, and gradually became so cursed by liquor that when he finally dropped into our Life Boat Mission in Chicago he had been drinking steadily for eight days. During that time he had not removed his clothing, nor had he sat down to eat a meal.

The strains of sweet gospel music that were wafted into the street through the open door of the mission reached his benumbed brain. Someone invited him in.

He thought it would be a chance at least to sit down in a chair and rest, so he went in.

When the invitation was given, he gave his heart to God. The spirit of God impressed him that he must also give up tobacco, to which he was more a slave than to liquor. This poor degraded wanderer said, "Yes, Lord, if you will help me, I'll give it up." Then he began to pray, and a new peace and assurance came into his life. As he walked out of the mission that night he threw his pipe and tobacco into the gutter, saying, "There's where you belong." He later became a faithful missionary nurse and led many others to the foot of the cross.

Amid all his medical work, teaching, and many lecture engagements over the country, David Paulson occasionally found time to drop in at the Life Boat mission meetings on State street in Chicago. One night the hall was filled with vagrants, drunks, and all sorts of men who were down and out.

As the meeting progressed, the attention of everyone became centered on a man in the audience who was talking loudly but incoherently. Slightly stooped, he looked to be past fifty years of age, with the all-too-well-recognized demeanor of the hopeless drunkard. Every line of his face spelled despair, and his gray eyes told of the agony of his heart. He evidently had no thought of finding hope there in a mission—just wanted a warm, comfortable place to rest.

David quietly left the platform and slipped in beside this man who was disturbing the meeting. Taking him by the arm, he said, "Come on, brother, we'll go upstairs." Once seated in a room upstairs, David said,

"My man, you know you're a slave to a bad habit. Don't you want to be free from it?"

"It's no use, Doctor, I've been a drunkard for nearly forty years. You can't do anything for me."

"You're right, man, I can't," said David, "but there's a God in heaven who can free you from this terrible habit. If you'll get down on your knees with me, we'll talk with the Lord about it."

"I don't want to pray," he said. "Nobody can help me. It's too late for me."

Succeeding in getting him on his knees, David earnestly prayed the Lord to deliver him from the liquor habit. Then the doctor said, "You must pray."

"I can't; I don't know how," he stammered brokenly.

"Just ask the Lord to deliver you from the liquor habit." The dejected, rum-soaked fellow finally blurted out these words, "Lord, if you can do anything for a poor broken-down bum like me, I wish you would, Amen."

In telling that story Dr. Paulson said, "That didn't sound much like a prayer to me, but evidently God heard a better prayer from the poor man's heart, for he rose from his knees apparently sober. I took him down again to the meeting, intending to see him when it was over, but he slipped out.

"Six weeks later he came back well dressed. 'I want to see the doctor with whiskers,' he said. I wasn't there that evening, but when it came time for testimonies that man stood up and told this story while the audience listened intently. He said:

" 'Six weeks ago I came into this mission a drunken outcast. My wife had left me in despair, my employer had fired me, and all my tools had been pawned for whisky. That doctor got me down on my knees, and something happened to me. I went right out and hunted up my wife, promising to give her no further trouble if she would come back to me. I told my employer I would stay sober if he would give me my job back and help me get some tools. It has been six weeks, and I still have no desire for whisky.' "

That man had gotten some pollen from another world, and it had fertilized his soul. That is what every person needs.

The doctor's observation was, "There are jewels hidden in all this moral rubbish. God's providential hand has been seen in so many different ways that it is clear our work for perishing humanity is ordered of Heaven."

Dr. Paulson felt that doing rescue work in a city like Chicago was like searching for pond lilies in a marsh—an infinite number of reeds and rushes for each lily. It requires diligent effort to find the lilies. When he has found himself, the new convert must receive constant encouragement until established in the new life. To strengthen their faith, these men were encouraged to begin at once helping others by telling their own experiences.

The doctor often drew word pictures of the poor men of the gutter and contrasted them with those of us who have been saved from such degradation. He said:

"One time a man had fallen through the ice, and some people were trying to help him out by thrusting a plank at him. But the board became so icy that each time he tried to take hold of it his hand slipped off.

Finally he gasped, 'For God's sake give me the warm end of the plank.' When they thrust him the other end of the plank his hand clung to it, and he was saved. Perhaps you and I are constantly holding out to people the frozen end of the plank. If so, may God help us to extend to them the warm end."

Another time Dr. Paulson said: "I remember that several years ago there was a woman drowning in Lake Michigan while two hundred men and boys stood on the wharf, any one of whom could have rescued her. One stole her pocketbook and all were criticising the lifesavers, who were trying to reach the spot. Not one of those two hundred attempted to pull her out of the water. I don't wish to be lined up with that crowd in the judgment.

"While in Chicago I learned more fully than I ever knew before that people whose lives are given up to self-sacrificing labor for others, experience the influence of it in their own lives. My work in Chicago brought me much in contact with earth's downcast. I have struggled with morphine cases—I have knelt down beside their beds and asked God to pity them, and I have seen these poor sufferers go off quietly to sleep, and to tell me afterward, 'Doctor, that was a most wonderful experience.' "

So Dr. Paulson entered fully into the joy of service for God. Though his purse was not apparently enriched from his years of service, yet his faith was strengthened and he understood what it meant to take God in as a partner.

CHAPTER TEN

A Trip to Europe

Dr. Paulson became a national lecturer on the gospel of health and salvation. He never lost sight of that vow he made to his Maker when near seventeen years old. He was a sick lad, and was facing death when he vowed, if spared, to give his life to help humanity both physically and spiritually.

In 1903 he was asked to spend three months in Europe. A series of conferences and other important meetings were to be held in the different countries, to which he could contribute much from his enthusiasm for truth and his wealth of experience. He prayed earnestly about making such an extended trip.

He said, "I had always wanted to go to Europe, but when brought face to face with the opportunity, my attachment for the work in sin-cursed Chicago far overbalanced it. But I went. I somehow felt in my bones that when I should come back I would be able to accomplish more for Chicago than I could by staying at home."

When, four years before, David and Mary Paulson arrived in Chicago with a class of forty students, he was asked to serve on the editorial staff of the *Life Boat*. W. S. Sadler was editor in chief at the time. Associated with him were M. E. Olsen, W. B. Holden, M.D., and

E. H. Hibbard. With Dr. Paulson there were then five members on the staff.

During 1903 W. S. Sadler and his wife, Lena Kellogg Sadler, withdrew from their major responsibilities in the mission, including his duties as editor of the *Life Boat,* that they might both enter the study of medicine. David then became editor in chief.

About that time some changes were made in the housing and conduct of the mission. Dr. and Mrs. Paulson took charge of the branch sanitarium on the south side of Chicago. The building on Wabash Avenue, which was commonly called "1926," was abandoned, and another large four-story brick building near the branch sanitarium was leased for a dormitory, with the *Life Boat* offices on the main floor. Here conditions were more livable, with a park and the shores of Lake Michigan only a few blocks away.

The doctor then had several stenographers and office assistants and had recently secured the services of a capable young woman to help in the *Life Boat* office. Years later I met her, and we were talking about Dr. Paulson and his characteristic ways of doing things. She said, "I shall never forget one thing he did back in those days."

"What was that, Lily?" I questioned.

"He was giving a lecture in a church on the south side of Chicago, and was talking so fast and saying so much all at once that his audience was having difficulty trying to follow him."

"What did he do that made you remember the incident for nearly fifty years?"

"When he noticed me sitting in the audience he

Top: Dr. Barnardo of London, "Father of Nobody's Children."
Bottom: Orphan Girls' Village, founded by Dr. Barnardo.

stopped talking in the middle of a sentence, looked toward me, and said, 'Lily Holiday, I want to see you after the service.' Then he went right on with his lecture."

I had to smile at Lily's description of the incident, because it was so like him. I said, "I have a feeling that while he was lecturing he thought of a place for you to connect with the work."

"You must be right, for that's how I happened to get a job in his office," she said.

When Dr. Paulson left New York for Europe he carried with him hundreds of copies of the *Life Boat,* which he handed out freely to the passengers on the ship. Thus he made some valuable contacts. One was a close relative of Jacob Riis. David had read the book *The Making of an American,* and had followed closely the noteworthy work of Jacob Riis and Theodore Roosevelt in cleaning up the slums of New York City.

As a result of this contact on the ship there sprang up an interesting correspondence between Jacob Riis and Dr. Paulson that proved valuable in bringing about an answer to prayer. It was only a year or two later that application was made for a change in the postal entry of the *Life Boat* from Chicago to Hinsdale, Illinois. But the postal department at Washington had just passed a new ruling refusing entry to a certain class of applicants. By a mere accident the *Life Boat* was caught in that class, and came under the proscription. Dr. Paulson made it a matter of special prayer. The thought came to him to write to Jacob Riis, whom he knew to be a close friend of President Theodore Roosevelt, and of George B. Cortelyou, Postmaster General.

In a short time he received a permit to publish the *Life Boat* from Hinsdale.

While in London Dr. Paulson studied the wonderful methods of the Salvation Army and met Gen. William Booth, its founder. He also visited other famous charitable organizations in England and on the Continent, being anxious to gain added knowledge for his work in Chicago.

Near London he found Dr. Barnardo's home for children with a family of ten thousand "nobody's children." Innumerable cottages housed its swarm of neglected youngsters. A needy child was never turned away. When the children were old enough to take positions in the world, they went out armed with a common school education and a trade. Barnardo's work was supported entirely by faith.

Paralleling Dr. Paulson's early experience, Dr. Barnardo also dedicated his life to medical missionary work. While studying medicine in East London he spent Sundays and two nights each week teaching ragged urchins.

"This school," said Dr. Paulson, "was first conducted in an old donkey stable."

One night after the class a ten-year-old boy, Jim, typical product of the slums, with tears in his eyes, his face thin and drawn, his sleeves hanging in shreds, lingered by Dr. Barnardo's side and pleaded to be allowed to remain overnight in the donkey stable."

"Why don't you go home to your mother?" Dr. Barnardo asked.

"Ain't got no mother," the lad replied.

"Your father?"

"Ain't got no father."

"Where are your friends and your home?"

"Ain't got no friends. Don't live nowhere."

"Dr. Barnardo thought he was lying," said Dr. Paulson. The boy assured him that there were "heaps like me. More'n I could count."

Continuing, Dr. Paulson said, "Dr. Barnardo told me he persuaded Jim to guide him to the 'Don't live nowhere' quarters, whatever they might be. He was led to an old shed with an iron roof on which eleven boys lay sleeping, huddled together to keep warm. It was a bitterly cold night, yet they slept there in nothing but the rags in which they were clothed. The wretchedness of their lot disturbed Dr. Barnardo. The question, Why should these have nothing and I and countless others have all we need? burned into his soul.

"Jim wanted to take him to another lay, but Dr. Barnardo had seen enough for one night. That sight haunted him until he vowed to dedicate his life to the work of saving the street Arabs."

Fannie E. Bolton, the poet, caught a glimpse of that little waif in these words:

"There stood before Barnardo a little homeless waif
Who asked for love and shelter, for refuge warm and safe.
His face so wan and pallid, his eyes with tears so dim,
His rags all told Barnardo how much he needed him.

"And yet still more to prove him the generous lover said,
'Go bring a friend to tell me your need of home and bread.'
Alas the little figure drooped down in half despair—
He had no friend to favor, could find no refuge there.

"With sudden inspiration he raised his ragged sleeve,
And said in trembling accents, 'You'll prove my need by these,

If in my ragged garments, no wretchedness you read,
Why, then, indeed, Barnardo, I have no friend to plead.'

"At this the generous lover felt tears unbidden start;
The plea for help was echoed in his own tender heart.
He washed and clothed and fed him and gave him refuge safe
And proved himself thereafter a father to the waifs."

Dr. Barnardo was an efficient, intelligent-looking man of only thirty-four, yet he had been a father to fifty thousand children in the few years he had been engaged in that work,—fifty thousand young lives saved from crime of every description and from its attendant punishment—what an enviable record!

He told Dr. Paulson that all but 3 per cent of the boys and girls of his charge had made good. What an example of the effectiveness of earnest prayer!

"When I was in London," said David, "the work had already absorbed fifteen million dollars, and still they were dependent on the Lord from day to day for their daily bread."

Dr. Paulson wanted to visit several of the famous centers of medical research in Europe—the Pasteur Institute in France, Dr. Koch's laboratories in Berlin, and many others. He did, however, see Dr. Pavlov in St. Petersburg (now Leningrad) and learned more about his discoveries of the activities of the digestive glands.

The trip the doctor never forgot was the one from Berlin to Norway, where he was called to see a patient. This story I caught from one of his several lectures to the student nurses about his trip to Europe.

He had explicit directions on how to find the town in Norway. Once there, he was told to turn down a certain alley, then climb one flight of stairs.

"I was unprepared for the surprise I was to receive," he said. "When I knocked, the door was opened by a nurse whom I had helped train in Chicago. She invited me into her brother's treatment room. After her graduation she had returned to her home in Norway, and I had lost track of her. She taught her brother how to give hydrotherapy treatments, and here he was in this crude place with the only entrance from an alley, yet he was having wonderful success.

"His sitz bath was an ordinary barrel he had cut down. His full bathtub was a box he had built and caulked to make watertight. For his Turkish bath he had simply nailed some cloth on a frame that was fastened together at the corners. There was a similar frame above, with a hole cut out for the head. He would put his patient in this canvas enclosure, and turn on the steam from a homemade apparatus beneath.

"He had only his brawny, skillful hands and a big heart back of them to accomplish what he did.

"In that crude place I met the priest of the town, the schoolmaster, and the leading druggist. I asked them what they were doing there. 'Well,' they said, 'we could get no help elsewhere, and this fellow is curing us.'

"He was an honest, noble man—he would not have been more noble if he had had an elaborate outfit. His outfit was cheap, but he was not. I would rather have a good, honest man and a cheap outfit than to have an expensive outfit and a cheap man."

Dr. Paulson earnestly told his students in Chicago that they must be mighty workers and then they would do mighty things with even humble apparatus. He said further, "There is a great deal of God's work that does not have a halo over it unless the worker has it in his own soul. There's such a thing as knowing the mind of God. It is a truth that needs to be emphasized more today. You can teach people massage, and how to prescribe the right diet, but many shrink from acquiring an experience that enables them to know the mind of God. If they shrink from that, their enterprise must be written in failure, even though they are equipped with the most expensive outfit."

Dr. Paulson spent a full and interesting three months overseas, giving many public lectures, visiting places that would add to his store of knowledge in his field, and paying little attention to historic centers of general interest. He returned with an enriched experience—with his faith in God deepened. He brought with him two young women, Elizabeth Bentele, a German girl who entered medicine in the American Medical Missionary College, and Anna Svalgren from Sweden, who connected with the Chicago Medical Mission.

Through all his travels there was one problem ever with him. When he was alone it absorbed his attention. How could he provide a suitable institution in the country for the many, many patients who were knocking on the doors of the small branch sanitarium on the south side of Chicago? He also wanted a suitable place for the worthy sick poor. He made these projects a special matter of prayer, ever striving to carry out his vow to God. His trip abroad had enriched his fund of knowledge and better prepared him to carry on his work in Chicago.

CHAPTER ELEVEN

Home Again

In 1903, before Dr. David went to Europe, both he and Dr. Mary had transferred their activities to the branch sanitarium and were living out there. The day before Dr. Paulson's return home Dr. Mary called the head nurse to her office.

Without looking up, Dr. Mary said, "O Edna, I want a last-minute checkup with you, to be sure everything is all right before I leave for New York."

"All right, Dr. Mary."

"Just think, Edna, I'm going to see David tomorrow. These last three months have seemed like years to me." Then as she looked up at Edna Langley, "Why! what does this mean? You're all dressed up!"

"That's right. I'm going to the station with you," she grinned.

"Oh, good! What a relief. I'm so excited over meeting David that I have been afraid I might get on the wrong train or do something else just as unaccountable."

"Yes, I thought you'd need some help," Edna replied, still smiling. "Now, Dr. Mary, don't worry about a thing. The patients will be well taken care of. I'll see to that while you're gone."

"I'll not worry, Edna, as long as you're on the job. Remember that text in Esther 4:14 that David is always quoting to you, 'And who knoweth whether thou art come to the kingdom for such a time as this?' We all appreciate your faithful work."

Gathering up Dr. Mary's baggage, they hurried to the corner, where they climbed onto the Cottage Grove cable car, and were off clickety-click, clickety-click, for the downtown station.

After buying her ticket Dr. Mary boarded the train. "Good-by, my dear," she waved, "take care of everything at the sanitarium."

"That's a large order, Dr. Mary, but I'll do it," and Edna smilingly waved her good-by. "We'll be looking for you both soon."

In New York, Dr. Mary learned David's ship was two hours off schedule. Taking a seat in the waiting room, she watched the clock, wondering whether those two hours would ever end. When the ship arrived, her eager eyes scanned the concourse of people moving slowly toward the gangplank. At last David's face stood out in the crowd, and that moment his hand went up to wave. He rushed forward through the crowd, and they were soon in each other's arms.

"Just wait here, my dear, until I get a cab." When they were comfortably seated on the train, bound for Chicago, he began asking questions.

"How have you been?" With her assurance that she was well, he continued: "Now, Mamie, has anything new come up that I have not heard about?"

"I wonder, David, whether you got my last letter telling that Dr. Wolfsen is back with us at the sanitarium? Also that Dr. Colloran came back and is helping at the dispensary."

"No, I didn't get that letter, but I'm glad they are with us again. They are both good men. What else new has happened? Tell me everything."

"You know by this time that we are crowded with patients at the sanitarium."

"You mean, my dear, that the sanitarium is full all the time?"

"Yes, indeed. Why, David, patients are so anxious to get in that we have to put up cots in our offices and in the corridors every night, and even let some sleep in the treatment rooms."

"Oh, you don't say!" he said, as his eyes beamed with enthusiasm. "I'm so glad to hear that. It means we'll be forced to build a sanitarium. We're going to build in the country, Mamie, but where and how?"

"That seems to be what is ahead of us. Have you any ideas?"

"Yes, I have, and I'm making it a special matter of prayer, as I know you are. Mamie, we must launch out into something more representative of the importance of our work, but I want to see the Lord's hand leading. We can't afford to make a mistake."

"It almost staggers me when I think of the money it will take to build a large sanitarium."

"Yes, it will take money, but the Lord is rich. The cattle on a thousand hills belong to Him. If we are in line with Providence, He will take care of the money."

"I believe all you say, but it's my faith that's short."

"But, Mamie, you must have more faith. Oh, look out the car window. Isn't the Hudson River beautiful!" They lapsed into silence as they gazed out the window at the broad sweep of the river.

"This is a beautiful trip," continued the doctor, "but I had more to say about our need of faith. That visit with Dr. Barnardo was a great inspiration to me. If the Lord can help him to care for ten thousand children a day over a period of many years, don't you suppose He will help us build a sanitarium to take care of sick people?"

"Yes, I know you're right. I'm back of you a hundred per cent, David, but there are times when I wish I could see the road ahead."

"But, Mamie, just recollect all our activities in Chicago and how many providences were shown us. The Life Boat Mission for instance."

He paused abruptly to comment on the tranquillity of the river.

"Yes, the river is beautiful," she said. "I can remember how, when a child, I enjoyed watching the thunderstorms roll down its course without apparently disturbing its calm progress toward the sea."

David called her thoughts back to his favorite topic —the mission in Chicago.

"Really, David, I have nothing new to report on the mission, only that they are doing a good work. They have a large crowd every night. Mr. Van Dorn is making good as a leader. He keeps the men interested."

"What about Fanny Emmel and Nina Crane, who are at the Life Boat Rest?"

"Oh, they are having wonderful experiences working for the girls in the red-light district on South Clark street."

"Are they still trying to support themselves by trusting entirely in God?"

"Yes, they are, David. They never come around to ask for any salary. Fanny said that they didn't worry about food when they had such a golden opportunity to save souls. She laughingly said the other day, 'Why should we worry when we always have dried beans and day-old bread. We'll never starve.' "

"Thank the Lord for such consecrated workers."

"You know, David, Fanny told me the other day that it was getting so she didn't have to pay streetcar

Facsimile of cover of the *Life Boat* magazine.

fare. Her work for girls has become so well known in that part of the city that even the conductors try to help her."

"The Workingmen's Home is filled all the time, I suppose?"

"Yes, indeed, and the men spend their evenings at the mission. I hear of wonderful transformations among them."

"What about the *Life Boat* magazine? Is the circulation up to 150,000 yet?"

"I think we are just a little past 150,000 in circulation now."

"You don't mean it! Thank the Lord for that."

"The sales agents' letters are very encouraging. You remember Miss Shields and Mae Coker?"

"Yes, they are the girls who started for San Francisco when I left for Europe and were going to earn their way by selling *Life Boats*. What success did they have?"

"They made it all right, and we're getting wonderful letters from them."

"You know, Mamie, every day I am more and more convinced that we need to strengthen our faith. It was worth my trip to Europe to meet Dr. Barnardo. The faith of that man staggers me. Why, my dear, we are just beginning to reach with our finger tips the great resources of God's power awaiting us."

"Yes, there are opportunities on every hand."

"We must put the best we have into the dough. If one has a cake of yeast, he must put it in the dough, and soon the whole mass will be leavened. Leaven does no good on the shelf. You and I know people who have five times more talent than we have, but they never get it working. They are too busy. Some say, 'Oh, yes, we have a gift for such things.' But their leaven is still in reserve. What we give away, Mamie, is what we keep. It is the seed that is yielded to the earth that comes back a hundredfold. Don't forget that."

"M-m-m."

"Of all things. Here I am rattling along and you sound asleep. Wake up, Mamie," he said, pulling her close to him. "You're sleeping your life away. You've been working too hard."

"Oh, no, David, I'm not worn out. You should know by now that I can always sleep when there's an opportunity. Have we passed Ann Arbor yet?"

"Yes, some time ago."

"I'll never forget Ann Arbor. We had good times that year, didn't we, even though we were studying for dear life at the university."

"Forget the past. We are living in the present. Tell me about the students in the medical college. Did any of them remain with us during the summer vacation?"

"Yes, David, a number of the students are with us. They are scattered around where needed, in the dispensaries, the clinics, and also at the branch sanitarium. We're certainly glad to get their help."

They lapsed into silence again as the train rumbled through the suburbs of south Chicago and smoothly glided into the Metropolitan area of the Loop. Suddenly the doctor began reaching for their baggage.

"Come on, Mary, we're pulling into Union Station right now. My, it's good to be back home."

CHAPTER TWELVE

Hinsdale—A Story of Prayer and Faith

It became more and more apparent to Dr. Paulson that he must find a location outside the city for a sanitarium. It seemed foolhardy for him to begin looking for a suitable property with no prospects of money to finance such a large project. But he did. That is, he began looking, and found two desirable places, but they slipped from his grasp while he was waiting for an indication of the Lord's approval. He continued to pray even though the outlook seemed discouraging.

One day C. B. Kimbell, a patient, came into his office for his usual checkup. Among other things, they talked about the charities David Paulson was interested in. Especially acute at the particular time were the growing needs in the work for girls on South Clark Street. Our nurses had gone into that district, rented a vacant store that had been used as a saloon, and then cleaned and painted it throughout. They furnished it as nearly like a home as they could, with carpets on the floors and lace curtains at the windows. They put out a sign, LIFE BOAT REST FOR GIRLS.

The district was nothing but saloons and brothels for many, many blocks. The only ray of hope in all that district was the electric sign over their door, which sent its beams out into the darkness.

"I'll tell you, Mr. Kimbell, our nurses don't know what to do with all those girls who come to them and insist on staying there. It's like leaving the fish you catch too near the water's edge. We must provide a place for them elsewhere."

"As you know, Dr. Paulson, I live in Hinsdale. That's seventeen miles out of Chicago. I have several residence properties out there. I'll let the nurses have one of those houses rent free for six months and a small rental after that."

"That's wonderful, Mr. Kimbell. I'll tell the nurses about it at once."

So it was that through the liberality of this prominent Chicago businessman, our rescue workers were given the use of a two-story residence in West Hinsdale. The cottage was soon filled with girls who were striving to return to a decent, normal life, entirely removed from the wicked surroundings in which they had been found.

Mr. Kimbell's frequent visits to the branch sanitarium for treatments developed his growing admiration for Paulson's simple faith and trust in God. They often talked about the crowded condition at the sanitarium in Chicago and the doctor's desire to establish an institution in the country where the patients could enjoy clean air and country life. Dr. Paulson sought Mr. Kimbell's advice concerning available property. One day Mr. Kimbell surprised him by saying, "Dr. Paulson, you ought to start a sanitarium in Hinsdale."

"Hinsdale, Hinsdale! why, I hadn't thought of looking out there for property."

"Well, it's a beautiful town only seventeen miles from Chicago, the home of many wealthy people."

"That's the trouble, Kimbell, Hinsdale is such a wealthy village the people might not want a sanitarium in their town, and besides, property there would be too high priced."

"Just the same, Doctor, I would like to see a sanitarium out there."

"So would I, Mr. Kimbell. That would be the ideal place for it."

Dr. Paulson was unprepared for the suggestion his visitor was leading up to. "I know of a piece of property that would be just the thing for you, and it's not too high priced," said Kimbell.

"You do?" The doctor's face lighted up. "That sounds good to me. Tell me about it."

"It's an abandoned ten-acre estate beautifully wooded, on rolling ground, with a large fifteen-room house, another smaller one of nine rooms, and plenty of outbuildings."

"That's better than anything I have heard yet." It was hard for the doctor to conceal his eagerness. "But the price, Mr. Kimbell?"

"Oh, forget about price until you see it."

"It sounds like an answer to our prayers. Anyway, I certainly want to look it over."

"Suppose you and your wife, Dr. Mary, come out to Hinsdale, and I'll take you all around the property."

Thus it was agreed, and in a day or two David and Mary Paulson took the train for Hinsdale. Mr. Kimbell met them at the station and drove up the hill, across the bridge, and over the railroad tracks.

"This is the southeast corner of the property on our left."

"Oh, this is wonderful!" exclaimed Dr. Mary. "What an expanse of lawn!"

"And there are plenty of shade trees," said David. "Oaks, elms, and maples."

"Look, David, a summerhouse just beyond the brow of the hill. How your patients would enjoy sitting there together in the shade on warm days." Her enthusiasm was rising.

"Sure enough. You see, Mr. Kimbell, my wife sees possibilities here already."

"I thought you'd both like it," he smiled. "Look across the street to the right. There are acres and acres of vacant property, sparsely wooded. You might want to buy all of that someday."

Judge Beckwith's residence on the ten-acre estate purchased for the Hinsdale Sanitarium.

"You may be a good prophet, Mr. Kimbell. I hope you are. If we could get this, the day may come sooner than we think when we'll be glad to have that acreage across the street as well as the ten acres here on our left."

Little did he know that in two years' time the sanitarium would purchase that sixteen acres to the east. Turning into the driveway to get a good view of the entire tract, Mr. Kimbell said, "Here we are, folks. This was the country home of Judge Beckwith, of Chicago. The place has been vacant for seven years. Times have changed since the judge's day. No one today will buy a private home with so much ground."

"No doubt that's true, Mr. Kimbell. It surely has been neglected, judging from the lush growth of weeds everywhere."

"Oh," Dr. Mary exclaimed, "the hill drops suddenly only a few feet from the rear of the house, and there's a ravine down there with water flowing through it."

"Yes, there is a ravine and there was formerly quite a brook down there, Dr. Mary."

"There are great possibilities here for us," said David, "and we'll not worry about the weeds."

"I'm glad you like it, Doctor. I feel this is a real providence for you."

"I feel the same, Mr. Kimbell."

"It all looks ideal for a sanitarium but where are we going to get the money?" put in Dr. Mary.

"My dear, where's your faith?" It was a typical question that the founder of Hinsdale Sanitarium often asked when the practical aspects of a problem confronted him.

"I guess, David, you have enough for both of us."

"I'm a believer in the use of nature's remedies. Patients should have fresh air, sunshine, suitable exercise, pure water, rest, a wholesome diet, a beautiful outlook, and a mind at peace with God and man."

"Well, Dr. Paulson, you could put all your ideas into practice on these grounds." Mr. Kimbell's voice was confident.

"I'm sure we could. In fact, it's ideal for our work. I'm afraid to inquire about the price the owners are asking for this property."

"Well, Dr. Paulson, hold your breath. They will sell the entire property for only sixteen thousand dollars."

"Sixteen thousand! You mean ten acres, these two large houses and several other buildings, all in a setting of picturesque grounds and trees for such a price! That's marvelous. We'll go home and pray about it."

And it really was marvelous, especially as we look at it today, fifty years later, when sixteen thousand dollars will scarcely buy a modest five-room house on a thirty-foot lot. But Dr. Mary was worried. When they left Mr. Kimbell at the station she turned to David and said, "Sixteen thousand dollars, David! That's a wonderful bargain, but we haven't a cent."

"That's all true, Mamie, but where's your faith?"

"Oh, guess I'm looking the wrong way again," she replied. "Anyway, it looks like a leap in the dark to me. I'm afraid my faith would waver if I were doing this alone, but I have confidence in your faith and am behind you a hundred per cent in going forward."

"I'll tell you, Mamie, it means that we must put

into this all there is of us. Essence of soul must be mixed with every work that endures through eternity."

"Well, I realize that this is vitally important work we have given our lives to, and God knows our hearts."

"Yes, you're right. If I were not interested in helping humanity, I would be a veterinarian. When a horse had colic or some other disease, I would correct it, collect my fee, and go home. That would be the end of it. But inasmuch as I am more than a horse doctor, I am interested in a larger ministry—one that can cure sick hearts as well as sick bodies."

"David, I feel the same about it."

"To tell you the truth, my dear, much as I like to see people cured of headaches, gastric ulcers, neuritis, rheumatism, and all the other physical torments, I would rather see people delivered from their sins. If I didn't feel that way, I might better be a horse doctor. When we reach the end of the journey we shall realize that to be saved from sin is the most important experience that could possibly come to us in this life."

"Oh, you're right, David, you're always right," she said as she grasped his arm.

"I knew I was right when I got you," he said with a smile. "Come, let's hurry and get home so we can call a meeting of the family tonight."

That evening an earnest prayer meeting was held. Dr. Paulson described in detail the property at Hinsdale; then all the enthusiastic group joined in prayer.

A few days later Mr. Kimbell came again to see the doctor. They talked quite at length over the various phases of the Hinsdale proposition.

"How did your prayer meeting come out, Doctor?"

"Well, I have nothing to report as yet."

"Paulson, I'll tell you what I'll do. I'll buy this property for you and deed it to you on the basis that you pay for it in twenty yearly installments without interest."

"Oh, how can we thank you, Mr. Kimbell? Why, you're answering our prayers. On this basis, I'm confident the Lord will help us to meet those payments. It's a go." So Dr. Paulson was fully convinced he was on the right track.

Now that the Lord had provided the land, plans were made during the fall and winter months for getting a small sanitarium started in the old Beckwith home in Hinsdale. The doctors had decided that someone else should head up the Hinsdale Sanitarium, inasmuch as they had no other thought than to remain in Chicago.

It was now February, 1904. Winter was nearly over. Something had to be done at once, for as yet no one had appeared to take charge of the Hinsdale project.

One day Dr. Mary said, "David, we'll have to go out there ourselves."

"Looks like it. That's just what I've been thinking. It reminds me of Elisha in Bible times. When he was asked to go heal a sick child he sent his staff by his servant to place it on the child's face. The servant went, but nothing happened. Elisha had to go himself before the child was restored."

They decided to go at once, and I was asked to precede them to get the house ready. Mrs. Fisk and Clyde Lowry, a young stenographer in our office, were sent along. Workmen were already on the place, and the cleaning-up job had begun. Doors and windows that had been carried off by tramps were replaced and the house made livable.

Did you ever taste the joys of pioneering for a good cause? I did. We pioneered even to cooking our meals over the coals in the furnace, for as yet there was no stove.

The following day David Paulson appeared. I remember that among other things he said, "What do you think? Some of my friends are beginning to joke about my coming out here to build a sanitarium without money."

"That doesn't disturb you, does it, David?" I asked.

"No; they even called me a lunatic, but I don't care what they call me as long as I'm following the Lord's leading."

"If they knew David Paulson as well as I do," I replied, "they wouldn't try to batter down the Rock of Gibraltar with nothing but their tongues."

"Well!"

"I'm right. That's just how determined you are when you know the Lord is leading you."

He turned to me with an air of confident assurance. "Caroline, you're going to see the day when those same people will be around humbly asking me for a job."

The doctor's prediction came true. I know that some of those people who ridiculed him did come back later and beg for a job. At the time of his death there were nearly three hundred employees in his sanitarium.

The fourth of March, 1904, was a dark winter's day when Dr. and Mrs. Paulson arrived in Hinsdale to make it their home. There was still some snow on the ground, which, because of a thaw the day before, had mingled with the mud, making it sloppy underfoot. Nature had done her worst to give these pioneers a cold shoulder. Even a neighbor's dog appeared and barked ominously at the intruders.

"David," said Dr. Mary as they were making their way up the hill, "this is hard walking in all this slush."

"Oh, I hadn't noticed. Just think how wonderful it will be in summer to have sick people scattered all over this lawn, basking in the sunshine."

In those days the street in front of the property was paved with blocks of wood. A wood sidewalk ran the entire length of the block. On the grounds there was one narrow wooden path, with boards missing here and there, leading from the main residence down the hill to the smaller (three-story and basement) servants' cottage, which the Doctors Paulson decided to occupy. Across the brook were the barns.

Directly beyond the rustic bridge was a two-story red-brick building—the most substantial-looking structure of all. Why Judge Beckwith, the owner, had favored the chickens to that extent I never found out. Perhaps it was Providence at work, for it took but little money and labor to transform that two-story brick chicken house into a dormitory for the workers, with a dining room and kitchen.

One of the first things Dr. and Mrs. Paulson did after coming to Hinsdale was to pray for the small sum of only one hundred dollars to clean up the grounds. Two days after that prayer a businessman whom David Paulson scarcely knew walked into Nels Paulson's office in Chicago and asked, "Does the doctor need some money out in Hinsdale?" Dr. Paulson's eldest brother, whom he had invited to join him in the work a few years before, slid forward in his chair as he said in surprise, "Does he need money! Why, he always needs money for his work."

The man pulled from his pocket a hundred dollars and handed it to Mr. Paulson. When Nels brought the money to Hinsdale, the doctor said, "That's quick returns. I rang up Central for that amount day before yesterday." Just a week later the man came back to Nels Paulson's office saying, "I felt impressed to bring another hundred for the doctor," and handed him a hundred-dollar bill. So David had another indication that the Lord was leading.

Shortly after this an elderly woman living in Chicago, whom Dr. Paulson knew slightly, sent for him. She said, "I just received twenty-five hundred dollars from a loan. Would you care to use it in your work in Hinsdale?"

"Well, my good woman, did you ever know of a time when I didn't need money for the work? Of course I need it, and thank you, and may the Lord bless you for answering our prayers."

When he returned to the office he told me, "I gave her my note for that. My stock is beginning to rise in the market. But I still have plenty of difficulties ahead."

It was a big venture—there were many anxious moments, but the work was progressing and he was fulfilling his vow to God. The darkest moments were always brightened whenever David Paulson prayed.

CHAPTER THIRTEEN

More Than Weeds Grew Here

The old estate of Judge Beckwith, which had stood unoccupied for seven years, came to life that first year that Dr. Paulson took over. The rank overgrowth of weeds that had taken possession of the property was beginning to give place to other signs of life.

The red-brick chicken house by the rustic bridge began to take on a new aspect. The original home of the judge was moved off its foundation a hundred feet or so to the north, and a wing of seventeen rooms was added north of that. Thus the most desirable building space in the center of the block was made vacant for the $100,000 building Mr. Kimbell said he would finance later.

In the fall of 1904 the Hinsdale Sanitarium and Benevolent Association was organized, with Mr. Kimbell as the first president. The organization was such that none of the employees, from Dr. Paulson down to the humblest callboy, could get a cent out of it beyond their salaries. The surplus, if any, was turned back into the institution. The same plan holds good today. Many thousands of dollars each year are spent in taking care of worthy sick poor.

It seemed an incredibly short time after the doctor arrived that a workman came running from the direction of the new dormitory across the bridge and hailed him.

"Hi, Doc!" he called.

Turning, the doctor saw the painter coming. "What's on your mind?"

"Doctor, I just wanted to tell you that I'll have the second floor of this building finished today."

"Are any of the rooms ready now?"

"Yes, two of them."

"Good! You're just in time. I'm on my way now to meet our first patient, and I didn't know where to put him. His mother is with him, so we'll need the two rooms. We'll have to use the dormitory until the main building is ready."

"All right," said the painter. "You'll have more rooms before night, Doc."

"We're going to have all these rooms filled just as soon as they are ready, brother. Keep moving. There's plenty of work ahead."

Early in 1905 Mr. Kimbell, who had gone to Glendale, California, to spend the winter, was suddenly stricken and passed away after a few days' illness. His arrangement for the property at Hinsdale was not changed, but no further help was received from his estate. It was a severe blow to Dr. Paulson. He had come to depend on Mr. Kimbell's wise counsel and judgment and looked to him for advice and guidance in financial matters.

The enormity of his obligations and his loss overwhelmed him. But only for a moment. There were many perplexing problems that continued to confront him, but each time he turned to God, his Source of strength, and found comfort. In strange ways help would come when needed, and often from some totally unexpected source.

One day later in the spring he said to his wife, "Mamie, I wish the roof was on the new wing. A patient may arrive almost any day, and we have no room ready."

"Well, David, why don't you hire more men to rush the job?"

"It's a question of a thousand dollars, not men, my dear."

"Well do I know it, David, but what can you do about it?"

"Do! I'll do as I always do. I'll call a meeting of the entire family tonight, and we'll pray for a thousand dollars."

To David Paulson the workers in the sanitarium were always "the family" from the very beginning, when there were not more than half a dozen, to the time of his death, when the family numbered into the hundreds.

All were present at that prayer service, even the children. The last one to pray was a nine-year-old boy who said simply, "Dear Lord, please send some money to the sanitarium."

The next day Dr. Paulson said to his brother Nels, "As I came up the hill this morning the conviction came to me that if I had drifted so far away that the Lord couldn't hear my prayer, He would hear the little shaver's prayer, and answer."

"It may be so." said Nels.

A few days later Dr. Paulson received a letter from a young man in Kansas. He wrote; "I hear you are trying to start a sanitarium in Hinsdale. I have just sold my farm and have $1,150 to place somewhere. I don't know why, but I feel urged to send it to you. Enclosed is my check for the amount mentioned."

On checking the postmark we found that the letter had been mailed the day after we had prayed.

It was only a matter of a few weeks when a bed patient arrived—all the way from Michigan. By this time the roof was on and a group of rooms were ready on the second floor—but the stairs were unfinished.

In the old part of the building there was a dumbwaiter that had evidently been used to carry furniture, trunks, and so forth, up and down. It was large enough to put a patient in it, stretcher and all. The boys pulled it up with a rope. So the patient rode to her room in style, a unique privilege that no other patient ever had. That young woman, invalided for years, soon went home cured and later became a physical culture teacher.

Dr. Paulson gathered courage from that experience. He said, "Like the first hundred dollars we received in answer to prayer, I took her restoration as an omen for good—as a sort of first fruits of a great army of invalids who were to follow and be restored."

The Nurses Training School opened July 5, 1905. It was a small beginning, and only four young women graduated three years later, but they were typical of the hundreds of missionary nurses who were to go out from that institution to various parts of the world, carrying the message of hope and freedom from both disease and sin.

Work was now moving rapidly on the new institution. Horace E. Hoyt, who was operating a health food cafeteria in Chicago, was invited to Hinsdale to be the business manager of the sanitarium. Olga Ziegler, a nurse who had graduated from the branch Sanitarium under the Drs. Paulson, became head nurse.

Government bonds were issued on the property, but it was hard to sell them with the sanitarium as security when there was nothing to show for them but an old residence with a new wing added. Dr. Paulson's faith was strong enough to bridge over his daily perplexities. He often said, "I see this entire lawn dotted with patients lying on cots and in wheel chairs, basking in the warm sunshine and the balmy breeze, drinking in health and vigor from nature itself."

One day a man stood at the threshold of Dr. Paulson's office door. "Why, if it isn't Omar Grantham! Come on in," the doctor said as he rose from his chair and shook hands with his visitor, whom he had met eight years before when on a lecture trip in a nearby State. Grantham had been persuaded to come to Battle Creek and train for medical missionary work, and was now on tour with a wealthy patron.

"I thought you were traveling over the world with that patient of yours. What brings you here?"

"We have been traveling, Dr. Paulson, but we're home for a while now."

"Has your patient been up to Battle Creek, lately?"

"Oh, yes, he always stops there for a few days when in the vicinity."

"Well, how does it happen you've stopped here? Have you something on your mind?"

"Yes, I have, Dr. Paulson. This patient of mine is interested in any good cause and has plenty of money."

"I'd like to meet him, Grantham."

"Yes, I want him to meet you and do something for your new sanitarium here. Would you meet him someday, soon?"

"Would I? Why, I'd make that my first concern. You see we're just at a stage where we find it difficult to sell our bonds when we have no institution in opera-

First nurses' class, Hinsdale Sanitarium, 1908.

tion as yet. Have him come to the branch sanitarium in Chicago and we'll have dinner together."

"How about Thursday this week if I can get him to come?"

It was so arranged, and with Mr. Emory Skinner Dr. Paulson met the dinner appointment at the branch sanitarium. While eating, the doctor told Mr. Skinner the interesting story of building a sanitarium on faith. "You see, this last spring we built a wing with seventeen rooms for patients, adjoining the original residence. Now we have to double our capacity."

"You mean you have to build again so soon?"

"That's just it. People are clamoring to get in. We want to get the foundation set before the ground freezes this winter."

"So you're after money."

"I am, Mr. Skinner. We have just issued some U.S. Government bonds, and we want you to buy five thousand dollars' worth."

"Oh, you folks are really a pack of grafters," he said smilingly. "They charged me seventy-five dollars a week in Battle Creek, and I didn't get much benefit, either."

With that Mr. Skinner got up and started for the door. "I don't want any of my money in your work," He shot back.

The man said it in a good-natured way, but the doctor admitted afterward that it was like a mustard plaster—no matter how good-naturedly it was applied, it began to raise blisters. His quick retort was, "When you get over on the other shore you'll wish you had some of your money in my kind of business. I'm going to do the work God wants done out in Hinsdale."

About six paces away Mr. Skinner turned and said, "Say, I rather like the looks o'your face. When you need that five thousand, let me know."

The doctor got his money.

Dr. Paulson with all his strong faith in his project and his power with God was handicapped with a weak body and fragile nerves, so that at times he was difficult to work with. Things had to move, and move quickly, around him. Yet I never saw Dr. Paulson lose his temper. I have seen his face flush when something was said that displeased him, but he never spoke an impulsive word to anyone.

He tried to instill that principle into his students and helpers, especially in dealing with sick people. One day the desk clerk got into an argument with a patient over his bill. The patient became angry. Word came to Dr. Paulson about the incident. The desk clerk was called to the doctor's office.

"What's the matter, John? Did you lose your head when dealing with that patient this morning?"

"Yes, I did, Doctor."

"He's angry and is telling that he's going home."

"I know, and I'm sorry, Doctor."

"Did you forget that in dealing with sick people the patient is always right?"

"I know that's what you have taught us, but the man was exasperating, and I forgot it at the moment."

"You must get that into your soul so you'll not forget again. The patient is always right, even though he's dead wrong. You've heard me say many times that God is the real manager of the Hinsdale Sanitarium.

When problems come that are too difficult for us to solve, we turn to God for help."

"Yes, Doctor, and your faith in the Lord has been a great help to me in my personal experience."

"You remember, John, not long ago when patients were going home improved or cured faster than new ones were coming in—we had special prayer and asked the Lord to send us twenty-five patients to fill these rooms in a week's time. We didn't ask for twenty-five people to get sick so they would have to come to us, but we asked the Lord to put it into the minds of twenty-five of all the hundreds of people about us who were carrying on their work with ailing bodies—people never without a pain or an ache—to come to Hinsdale for a few weeks to get rid of their suffering."

"Yes, Dr. Paulson, I remember it all. Twenty-five patients came before the week was up, and here I am sending them away."

"Why, John?"

"I think it was because I didn't start the day right. I have discovered that if I don't start the day with prayer, things get into a tangle before ten o'clock, as they did today."

"That's a good discovery, son. Keep on praying, and you'll be a valuable worker someday."

It was incidents like this that greatly endeared Dr. Paulson with his workers. With the blessing of God the sanitarium was growing rapidly. Opposition and prejudice were disappearing as Dr. Paulson was busy planting seeds of truth in the hearts of those he had gathered about him. It gratified him to realize that he was fulfilling his vow to God.

The Hinsdale Sanitarium, 1909.

CHAPTER FOURTEEN

Keeping Time With God's Clocks

To Dr. Paulson the important thing in his life was to keep time with God's clocks. Those first few years at Hinsdale were one round of praying and building, praying and building, as the providence of God led the way.

In the fall of 1906 another addition was under construction, which would for the second time double the capacity of the sanitarium. Only two years before he had begun to build a sanitarium with nothing but prayer and faith. It was Dr. Paulson's great desire to help sick and suffering humanity that led him to undertake so gigantic a task with no assurance of success but his undying faith and trust in God.

Finishing his list of patients one day, Dr. Paulson telephoned, "Give me Mrs. Paulson's office, please."

Dr. Mary's Hello came back immediately.

"Mamie, are you nearly through with your patients?"

"Yes, David, I hope. It's been rush, rush all day long here."

"I wish you would drop over to my office before we go home, please. I have something on my mind."

"All right, David, I'll be right there."

When Dr. Mary arrived he said, "Mamie, our business manager was just in. He says he has received fifteen letters in the mail today from patients who want to come at once."

"But there are no available rooms, are there?"

"Available rooms! I should like to see one! Mr. Hoyt says that for weeks we have had to make up cots in the treatment rooms and offices to accommodate the overflow."

"Yes, I know David, for someone has been sleeping in my office."

"Do you remember, Mamie, what Mr. Kimbell said before he died about building a large $100,000 sanitarium here on this hill?"

"How could I forget it! But that's all in the past. We can't plan on getting anything from the Kimbell estate now."

"I know we must look to the Lord and to the living to help us now. I hardly know which way to turn," he said as he nervously paced the floor.

"Neither do I, only to pray about it."

"Here we are," he said as he paused in front of his wife—"patients clamoring to get in—a new addition started but no money to finish it. I'm telling you, Mamie, we must get together for special prayer this very evening."

"You're right, David; that's the thing to do."

That evening our group of earnest workers in the Hinsdale Sanitarium—the manager, bookkeeper, desk clerk, callboys, supervisor, and all the nurses and domestics, in fact about forty or fifty people—met and took part in a season of prayer.

When we rose from prayer Mr. Hoyt said, "Dr. Paulson, may I say something?"

"Yes, go ahead, Hoyt."

"I feel impressed to see a woman who has already let us have a few hundred dollars."

"Very well, Mr. Hoyt," the doctor agreed, "you had better take the next train. That woman may not have any more money for you, but the Lord may have something else for you to do up there in Wisconsin. You may be able to plant some seed that will bring fruit later."

When Mr. Hoyt reached the home of their donor in Wisconsin, a pale, nervous woman answered his knock by opening the door a tiny crack and peeking out.

"Mrs. Van Houten?"

"Yes," she said as she nodded her head.

"I'm Mr. Hoyt from Hinsdale. May I come in?"

"I can't let you in. Please go away."

"But I've come all the way from Hinsdale, Illinois, to see you."

"I suppose you want some money," she said crustily. "I have none for you."

"But Mrs. Van Houten, it may be I can do something for you," he said smiling.

"For me? Well!" Reluctantly opening the door, she said, "Come in and I'll tell you. My husband is at home and he's intoxicated. When he's in this condition I never let anyone in."

"But I may be able to help him."

"This has been going on for many years, and I'm about worn out. Nobody can help him."

"I would like to talk with him."

"Oh, you can't do anything for him. I have lost all hope. It's gone on too many years."

With that a red-nosed, bleary-eyed man staggered into the room.

"Who are you?" he inquired.

"Oh, Mr. Van Houten? I'm Mr. Hoyt from Hinsdale."

"Sure, I know who you are. You have quite a wad of my wife's money down there."

"Yes, we have. May I have a little talk with you, Mr. Van Houten?"

"Well, come on in here. What do you want to talk about?"

They visited a bit, then gradually Mr. Hoyt turned the conversation to Mr. Van Houten, himself, and what he was bringing upon himself, and his wife, and friends because of his drinking. He invited him to accept Christ's invitation to all who were in his condition. "Come now, and let us reason together . . . : though your sins be as scarlet, they shall be as white as snow; though they be red like crimson, they shall be as wool" (Isa. 1:18).

Mr. Hoyt felt he was impressing the man as he saw the belligerent look fade from Mr. Van Houten's face and his muscles relax. The Lord was working on his heart. Mr. Hoyt suggested prayer. The poor man dropped to his knees. Both men prayed. Mr. Van Houten's prayer seemed earnest, right from the heart. He was tired of the old life and eagerly reached out for something better.

As they rose, Mr. Van Houten looked at Mr. Hoyt and pleaded, "Won't you make my wife promise to read the Bible and pray with me every day?" Quickly Mrs. Van Houten threw her arms around her astonished husband. They blended their tears of joy as she said, sobbing, "This is the happiest day of my life."

"It is of mine, too. I'm sick of the old life. I had about decided that my only hope was in God. I thank you, Mr. Hoyt. God sent you here at just the right time."

Mr. Hoyt expressed his joy at their reconciliation, and was pleased to hear Mrs. Van Houten say, "Van, we're going to pray and work together the rest of our days."

That drunkard's home had suddenly cleared of all the fog, and the gloom had changed to a glow of hope. The drunkard had changed masters—broken the shackles of evil, and was free once more, free to obey the Lord with a clear conscience. The look of despair on Mrs. Van Houten's face a short hour before, when she told Mr. Hoyt that her husband was a hopeless drunkard, had now changed. Her whole attitude was one of confidence in her husband's resolution.

Mr. Hoyt, too, left the home with a lighter step although, with no thought of the financial troubles that brought him there, he realized he had kept time with God's clocks. By the time he reached home he had developed a sense of regret that he could not bring a sum of money to Dr. Paulson, but as he told his story, Dr. Paulson said: "Hoyt, you have sown the seed. God will take care of the harvest. The farmer plants his corn in the spring. He knows he has to wait until fall for the harvest. We must not attempt to push the Lord into answering our prayers at once. He knows best."

"Yes, Dr. Paulson, I realize I have been impatient.

I wanted to bring the harvest back on the train with me today."

"That's natural, Hoyt, but you'll reap a harvest in the soul of that man, and you'll have your reward."

"That's something, Doctor."

"While you've been away I paid a visit to the mason in the village and persuaded him to do our cement work on a time contract. He said we could have three years to pay him."

"Good, I'm glad to hear that."

"I must say, Hoyt, the mason would have shown good sense if he had hesitated to agree to the request, but he didn't."

"That'll be a big help, Doctor. We can swing it as long as the patients continue to flock in as they are doing now."

"But, Hoyt, you know we are also getting small amounts of money through the mail for our building fund—some has come in while you were away."

"Oh, I'm glad to hear that, too."

"My faith is in God, Hoyt. I believe He will not forsake us."

When completed, the new addition made a total of forty guest rooms. That very summer I remember we had fifty-six patients at one time. Again beds were set up in the offices and there were several people on the waiting list begging to be admitted.

"Again we prayed God to show us," said the doctor, "whether we should, in our poverty, attempt another enlargement or build some cottages."

The cottages were decided on, and four patients in the sanitarium were each willing to build a cottage and live in it while there under treatment. In a short time the sanitarium owned all four cottages, and they soon became valuable as homes for married help.

In 1907 our country was passing through a period of financial stress, which had its effect on the sanitarium. A man in Chicago who had loaned the Doctor two thousand dollars wrote that he had decided to build a home for himself and was coming out on a certain day to get his money. The doctor said: "We were not prepared to pay that two thousand to him, so a group of us got together in my office and prayed the Lord to change his mind and convince the man that he didn't need the money. Sure enough, when the man arrived he decided that he wouldn't build at all, so left his money with us.

"Some people who had loaned money to the sanitarium subject to demand also wanted their money at once. This called for further prayer, and the Lord helped us through it all."

Nine months passed before the Wisconsin couple were heard from again. Then came a letter from Mrs. Van Houten saying her husband had been a sober man all those nine months, but now she was worried. He had gone to New York City to settle up the estate of a brother who had recently died under very disgraceful circumstances. This brother had been a black sheep in the family. In closing her letter she said, "I'm imploring you people in Hinsdale to do something to help my Van right now."

When that letter arrived, Dr. Paulson, being familiar with the dangerous district in New York where this brother lived, decided that both he and Mr. Hoyt should go at once. Dr. Paulson said, "I know what Mr. Van is up against, because I lived in Dr. Dowkontt's mission home near there while taking my senior year in medicine."

They boarded the Twentieth Century Limited for New York, but not without first seeking God earnestly for guidance. I remember that prayer service, when our sanitarium family, about fifty, assembled in the gymnasium. Many prayers ascended to the throne of God in their behalf.

Arriving at the address given, they knocked on the door. A wan, haggard, suspicious-looking woman answered.

"We want to see Mr. Van Houten," said Mr. Hoyt.

"He is not here," was the reply.

Dr. Paulson spoke up, "Please go up and tell Mr. Van Houten that Dr. Paulson is here from Chicago to see him."

They were shocked at how quickly the woman left to obey orders. She returned, saying, "All right, he is ready for you. Third floor, second door to the right."

"There we found Mr. Van Houten," said Dr. Paulson, "with a sharp lawyer who had succeeded in getting him intoxicated and was at that moment procuring his signature to papers signing away to others his brother's wealth. Ten minutes later his signature would have been attached to those bogus papers and the lawyer gone. God's clocks keep time."

Mr. Van Houten told the men that his brother had left everything to him and had made him the executor of his estate. In the brother's safe they found some fifty thousand dollars and other valuables. Mr.

Hoyt took care of the legal proceedings and a happy Mr. Van Houten returned to his equally happy wife and their quiet Wisconsin home.

This dear old couple lost no time in making out a will leaving all they possessed, as well as the brother's estate, to the Hinsdale Sanitarium. In a few months Mr. Van Houten passed away—a Christian man.

Those of us who were present during that experience thought back only two years to the time when Mr. Kimbell, shortly before his death, advised the doctor to move the old main residence on the sanitarium grounds to the north so that the center of the ten acres on the hill could be left for a $100,000 building which he, Mr. Kimbell, would finance a little later, but his death put an end to that dream.

Dr. Paulson, undaunted, continued to work and pray, believing that when the need arose for a large new building the Lord would provide the means. Now, here in the Van Houten legacy was the larger part of the money available to build a new, modern sanitarium.

"I tell you," said Dr. Paulson, "it's a solemn thing to live. Things are not running loose in this world. God is leading. His plans will be carried out, but you and I must watch for opportunities. When such opportunities come to us to minister to others, if we neglect them, we meet with a greater loss than those who need our ministry."

While telling the experiences of this chapter in a lecture on the story of Hinsdale, Dr. Paulson said, "Grain that is not harvested when it is ripe falls off and is lost. So opportunities, when they are not eagerly grasped, speedily vanish, and neither prayers, tears, nor fasting can bring them back.

"There are many people who regard their religion much as the traveler at sea regards his life preserver—as a handy thing to have in case the ship should go down. They take religion just as they do medicine, not because they relish it, but because they suppose they need it.

"I feel that I cannot work a day without prayer for divine guidance and that power that keeps one's heart. God's spirit will guide you if you'll let it. The greatest thing in this world is a surrendered life. A man's ideas may be ever so good, but they are not worth a snap if he depends upon these alone. To be divinely led is the best thing in all the world."

CHAPTER FIFTEEN

A Bank That Never Failed

"Dr. Paulson, may I see you a moment?"

"Yes, Mr. Hoyt. Come in and be seated."

"Well, Doctor, how do you like our new building by now?"

"How do I like it?" The doctor straightened up with pride. "I think it's grand, Mr. Hoyt. Our dream for a $100,000 sanitarium is almost a reality. The interior finish and furnishings are elegant."

"I believe this new building will draw a higher class of people to our sanitarium."

"Yes, you're right, Hoyt; Hinsdale certainly needs this sanitarium. The wife of the Armenian ambassador here means much to us now. Mrs. Paulson is her physician, as you know."

"Yes, I met the ambassador when he brought her here the other day. They are nice people."

"I tell you, Hoyt, it gives us prestige to have such prominent people with us. One thing I see in it—prosperity means more funds to care for the sick poor. You know the poor are always in my mind."

"You're right, Dr. Paulson; but what I want to talk with you about is the same old story." His face took on a sober, anxious look as he asked, "Where can we borrow more money?"

"What's the situation to date, Mr. Hoyt?"

"Well, the biggest problem is that we still owe the contractor some ten thousand dollars. He said that if he had five thousand now to pay his help he could wait a while for the balance."

Ten thousand dollars to raise in a few months! It looked like an impossible sum to acquire in so short a time, but when starting the sanitarium in Hinsdale Dr. Paulson remembered praying for a hundred dollars at first, and it came. Then his faith was strengthened, and he prayed for more—every need was met. He even prayed for a thousand at one time, and that prayer was answered. Now there was ten thousand needed—would his faith reach that?

Yes, he would pray, but there was Mr. Hoyt—he must be encouraged to have faith.

"Well, Hoyt, do you have any suggestion as to where we could get this money?"

"No, Doctor," shaking his head, "I haven't; only old Dr. Pearsons comes to my mind."

Dr. Pearsons was a retired multimillionaire living in the village of Hinsdale who, having no heirs, was placing his millions with educational and other public institutions for the betterment of humanity.

"You know, Dr. Paulson, I think Pearsons with his six million ought to spare a little to help a struggling sanitarium to get on its feet, especially when the institution is right in his own town. Don't you think?"

"That sounds plausible, Hoyt; but I've been told that Dr. Pearsons is hard to approach." Then after a moment's hesitation he said, "But with the Lord's help I'll go see him right now."

Dr. Paulson strode over to the old mansion of Dr. D. K. Pearsons, and did his best to convince the ninety-year-old doctor that it would be a privilege for him to help the sanitarium with a loan of only five thousand dollars. No one knows how he got it, but he came back with the check.

A few months later another five thousand was needed. "By that time," said Dr. Paulson, "the old doctor was a patient in the sanitarium and had decided to remain there the rest of his days. When I asked him for a second five thousand, the answer was, 'The trouble with you, Paulson, is you keep the sanitarium too warm. If you didn't waste so much on coal, you would have money to build without borrowing."

Dr. Paulson finally convinced him that sick people needed more heat than well people. He got his money when he promised that he would pay all ten thousand back by April first. That was during the holidays. Two weeks before April first the old man came tottering into Dr. Paulson's office. "Say, Paulson, you got that ten thousand yet?"

"Well," said the doctor, with a smile, "No, I haven't. I had hoped you would forget about that for a while."

"I haven't forgotten. I want that money for one of the colleges Governor Deneen is interested in. Do you know where to go for the money?"

"No, I don't right now," said the doctor. Noticing a look of disappointment—almost anger—on the old man's face, he said, "Do you think the college needs it more than we do?"

"But I've promised Governor Deneen," he shouted.

"If I had only known you couldn't pay it back, you never would have gotten a cent from me."

"I can get it, Dr. Pearsons."

Eagerly he inquired, "Where?"

"I'll look to the Lord for it, where I usually get an answer—from the bank that never fails."

There was a distressed look on old Pearsons' face that indicated he wished Paulson had a more satisfactory place to look, but he said nothing.

Thursday was the first of April, and by Monday, just three days before, Dr. Paulson still had no money for the old man. "Tuesday morning," said Dr. Paulson, "when I finished conducting morning worship for the patients, a woman who was visiting friends in the institution, whom I had not even met, came to me and said, 'Dr. Paulson, while we were singing in the parlor this morning a thought came to me. I am expecting five thousand dollars in the morning mail. Perhaps you can use it.' "

"Oh, yes, indeed, I can use it. That will answer my prayer."

"You mean you have been praying for this money?"

"That's true, my good woman; I have been praying. Did you say five thousand?"

"Yes, it is five thousand I'm expecting."

"I can't tell you how pleased I am to get that, but it is ten thousand I have been praying for, which I must have on Thursday of this week."

"I'm sorry, Doctor," she meekly replied; "It is all I have for you."

After the woman left, Dr. Paulson stood alone by the window in his office, his left hand hanging by the thumb from his pants' pocket—a characteristic pose. He was thinking, "Why did the Lord send only half the amount we prayed for? It isn't like the Lord. He usually answers our prayers with an abundance. When we prayed for a hundred dollars to clean up the grounds, the Lord sent two hundred. When we needed a thousand dollars for the roof, God sent $1,150. He must have something else in store for us. We'll wait, and continue to pray." With that thought he sat down again at his desk.

A few hours later Dr. Pearsons came in. "Say, Paulson, if you folks can dig up five thousand, I can tell you where to get the other five."

"We already have the five thousand."

"What! You already have the five thousand?" The aged doctor was surprised.

"Yes, the Lord sent it this morning."

"Well, you and the Lord must be in league with each other."

"I've learned by experience that the Lord does answer prayer, Pearsons."

"That's good. Now this must be another answer to your prayer—I've been down to the bank and told them that you were nice people and that they should do business with you folks here on the hill. They said they would, and promised to let you have five thousand dollars now."

"I most surely think this is another answer to my prayer. Thank you, Dr. Pearsons."

Not for one moment did David Paulson forget his promise to the Lord to take care of the sick poor and unfortunates of earth. When the Hinsdale Sanitarium was organized some four years before, he declared his aims and purposes to the board at their first meeting. He made this statement from the depths of his heart, "Unless you are going to help me do something for the sick poor of earth, there is no use to go on. I am determined there shall be one spot left on this selfish earth where a man can have a helping hand extended to him whether he has money or not. I shall see to it that this whole tract of land is filled with the sick of earth, and we shall minister to them the healing forces of nature."

At that first board meeting the newly appointed president, Mr. Kimbell, had said, "I'm interested in the poor —I am also interested in the rich. Why not build a sanitarium first for those who can pay; then when we get under way we can establish a work for the sick poor."

Dr. Paulson, after thoughtful consideration, reluctantly agreed to that policy. Although he didn't have a separate building for the poor at the start, he never turned away a needy case. As a result, at the end of each year there were thousands of dollars written off the books to charity.

On the property east of the sanitarium stood a frame building containing fourteen rooms which Dr. Paulson, in 1910, decided to remodel, furnish with plain, simple furnishings, and equip for a sanitarium for the poor. It was called the Good Samaritan Inn.

In this building "patients could get basement bargains in health who could not afford the high-priced accommodations at the sanitarium across the street." The sick poor were treated on such a simple yet effective basis that it was within their reach. They had the same doctors, the same good food, the same nursing, and the same personal interest in their cases.

In 1902 the Chicago Medical Mission suffered a serious loss caused by the disastrous burning of the Battle Creek Sanitarium, which resulted in the cutting off of the financial support the mission had been receiving.

In 1910 the American Medical Missionary College closed its doors in favor of the College of Medical Evangelists in Los Angeles, which was getting a healthy start as a medical school, operating under the same principles that brought the Chicago institution into existence. All the clinics and dispensaries carried on under the Chicago Medical Mission were closed.

Dr. Paulson had already transferred his interests to Hinsdale, with the burden of Chicago's poor still on his heart. At Hinsdale he now had three institutions —the sanitarium, the home for girls, and the Good Samaritan Inn for the sick poor.

The doctor then established a city visiting nurses' service. Each nurse in training was required to spend a stipulated number of weeks caring for the sick poor of Chicago, visiting in their homes, helping to conduct services in the jails. This led to many unfortunate girls being released or paroled by the courts to our social workers, who would bring them to the Life Boat Rescue Home in West Hinsdale, where they were under the care and protection of our matron, Mrs. Hannah Swanson, and her assistants.

The small dwelling house in West Hinsdale soon became too small to accommodate the girls. Dr. Paulson, on visiting this home one day, discovered that there were at least three girls or more crowded into each bedroom. He said to the matron, "Mrs. Swanson, this crowded condition must not go on. We must build a new rescue home for girls, large enough to take care of all the girls who come to us, and we must do it right away."

"Dr. Paulson, that's an answer to our prayers. Not only have we prayed, but we have been saving every cent we could for this purpose. Our only income has been donations and the small pittance of board money we have received from the girls themselves."

"How much is there in your fund?"

"I think it is around a thousand dollars by now."

"A thousand dollars! My, you folks must have economized to the limit to get that much ahead."

"But, Dr. Paulson, we learned that years ago when we were in Chicago on South Clark Street at the Life Boat Rest. We found then that we could get along nicely on the gifts that were sent in."

"Well, my dear woman, I want to tell you that with the Lord's help we'll build one of the best homes for girls in the State of Illinois. That thousand dollars will pay for the land."

When Dr. Paulson returned to his office that day he told me what he had decided to do. I knew we were facing another campaign for funds, and I was glad to help. This time all the money must come as gifts and donations to a charity. The need had developed into a crisis. This was in 1908-9, when the new large sanitarium was still under construction.

The doctor, without hesitation, acted at once. A

small plot of ground was purchased four and a half blocks northeast from the sanitarium, on Philipa Street. A meeting of the sanitarium workers was called. A few patients came who had asked for the privilege. The purpose of the proposed project was clearly stated to the fifty or more present. Stress was laid on the urgency of the need. An earnest season of prayer followed.

The majority of the group were employed by the sanitarium at a small wage, yet everyone responded with gifts and pledges. Nine hundred dollars was raised. I remember one patient who was a neighbor, a retired physician, who gave one hundred dollars. The rest was in smaller sums.

The next thing Dr. Paulson did was to call a mass meeting in the village. He had the cooperation of the pastors, civic authorities, and women's clubs of Hinsdale and nearby villages. The invitation to the meeting was signed by the presidents and chairmen of the various organizations, and also by the pastors. Dr. Frank Gunsaulus, the great pulpit orator of Chicago, gave an inspiring address in the Hinsdale clubhouse.

Some forty people, many of them among Hinsdale's millionaires, each gave a hundred dollars, besides the gifts from many others.

I cannot remember the names of all those generous-hearted people of Hinsdale who responded to the appeal for funds. Mr. Frank O. Butler, owner of the large J. W. Butler Paper Company of Chicago, was one who through the years continued to lend his support and his influence to the work for wayward girls who came to this home.

Mr. Kroehler, of Naperville, a few miles away, was

another generous contributor. There is scarcely a furniture store of any size in all the country today that does not sell Mr. Kroehler's furniture. When we needed some overstuffed furniture for our living room, to make it more presentable for the dedication, as none had come in, we visited Mr. Kroehler, with whom we were acquainted, the day before the dedication. A beautiful set of parlor furniture was rushed to us promptly in time for the services. Dr. Paulson was delighted to find that more people had sent money to furnish rooms in the home than there were rooms to furnish.

He visited the rebuilt Battle Creek Sanitarium to raise money for the home and came away with some thousand dollars from a lecture he gave while there. One incident on that trip warmed his heart. The next morning after his lecture he felt impressed to visit the mother of one of the sanitarium doctors. He didn't know why, because that was the only private home he visited.

The woman came to the door in answer to his knock, and after greeting him said, smiling, "I know what you came for—to get twenty-five dollars from me."

"How did you happen to know that?"

"Oh, I attended your meeting yesterday."

"I don't understand. What made you think I would come here to your house?" he inquired.

"Well, I promised the Lord if He sent you here I would give you twenty-five dollars."

Another experience the Doctor often liked to tell was about his St. Louis trip. He received a request from a sick woman there to come to see her. She would pay him well for making the trip. He replied that he was sorry he couldn't spare the time to go that distance, 350 miles, to see one patient. She would have to come to him. The fact that he could make some extra money for himself made no impression on his mind.

She answered immediately that she was too sick to make the trip. If he would come, she would give a hundred dollars toward building the rescue home. He took the next train. He found she was beyond human help, but he had prayer with her and came back with two hundred dollars for the home.

Sufficient money came in to complete the four-story building, containing thirty rooms, and to dedicate it free from debt in 1909.

Girls were sent to this home, not only from Chicago but from all the Great Lakes district. Often we were told, "You people surround these girls with a strong spiritual influence that changes their lives. As probation

The Life Boat Rescue Home for Girls, 1925.

officers and social workers, we notice the difference in them."

In all, some sixteen hundred girls were sheltered in that building, which remained open for twenty-five years after Dr. Paulson's death. I heard Dr. Paulson say at one time that nearly 90 per cent made good after leaving the home.

Dr. Paulson opened a branch of the Hinsdale home for girls in the old branch sanitarium in Chicago, which had been standing idle for some time. He placed Mrs. Swanson and Mrs. L. A. Wade in charge. The building was large. There were many rooms to heat. It was winter, and their coalbin was almost empty. Mrs. Wade told Dr. Paulson of their critical situation. "Doctor, what shall we do? We are out of coal and have no money. We can't let our girls suffer."

"What do you want to do about it, Mrs. Wade?"

"Well, I wish we had a hundred dollars so we

Orphans of the Life Boat Rescue Home, 1925.

could buy a carload of coal at one time. We could save a lot of money that way."

"Then why don't you go to headquarters? Ask the Lord for a hundred dollars to buy coal."

"What, pray for coal?" she said.

"Yes, why not? Don't you suppose the Lord knows the coalbin is empty?"

"Of course, why not? We will pray."

"I'll pray about it too." he said.

A few days passed, and a letter came from an elderly person down State, written in a shaky hand—just three lines: "I feel impressed you need a hundred dollars for your work in Chicago, so I'm enclosing it herewith."

The doctor took that letter and the hundred dollars to the workers in Chicago. Tears came to their eyes as they realized that so quickly the Lord had answered their prayer in a definite way, even for such a common thing as coal.

"The trouble with some folks," said Dr. Paulson, "is that their prayers are so general that if they were answered they would never know it. If they were not answered, they would never miss it."

He didn't believe in keeping his religion and his daily life in separate compartments. He felt sorry for people who treated their religion like their good coat—to be hung in the closet and worn only a few hours each week. He felt they were living miserable, narrow lives when they could be living full, noble, joyous lives.

Dr. Paulson had discovered the key to the bank that never failed, and he would often draw on that bank, never for himself, but to help others.

The new Hinsdale Sanitarium, 1955.

CHAPTER SIXTEEN

A Glimpse of David's Prayer Life

I have said nothing so far about Dr. Paulson's prayers for the recovery of the sick. He was always reticent about mentioning the results of such prayers.

Fifty years ago there were numerous so-called faith healers who were merely carrying on a racket and advertising far and wide their "miraculous" cases of healing. Dr. Paulson wanted none of that. His greatest joy was in seeing the patient restored to family and home with more faith in God.

When it seemed that the patient was beyond human help, then it was he prayed the Lord to interfere and restore the patient if it were His will.

Once I heard Dr. Paulson say that there are some people bound to regard these experiences with considerable skepticism, others who treat them lightly, and a still larger group who may be inclined to focus their attention on the instrument instead of recognizing the Hand that guided the instrument. This beautiful blending of human need with divine power lends significance to human existence and gives us courage and faith to depend implicitly on God's promises.

The chief surgeon in the Hinsdale Sanitarium some forty years ago was Dr. Franklin H. Martin, a prominent Chicago physician, editor of one of the largest medical journals in this country and director general of the American College of Surgeons.

I heard him tell at one time about his impression of Dr. Paulson when he came to perform his first operation in the Hinsdale Sanitarium. He said, "We stood by the operating table ready to begin our work. I was surprised when Dr. Paulson said, 'Wait a moment,' then he offered a simple, earnest prayer for the success of the operation and the life of the patient, asking the Lord to especially guide the hand of the surgeon. I will never forget that day. I learned afterward that this was routine for him, but it was certainly a new experience for me. Never before did we work so hard as my assistant and I did to make that prayer come true."

Many years later, when it was evident to Dr. Paulson's colleagues that his health was slowly but surely failing, Dr. Percy T. Magan, from Nashville, Tennessee, a close and warm friend of David's dating back to their college days in Battle Creek, was visiting the doctor at Hinsdale. Dr. Martin was again called to operate on a critical case. After the surgery was finished, the two men, Dr. Martin and Dr. Magan, took the same train for Chicago. They strolled along together toward the Highlands Station discussing Dr. Paulson's physical condition.

"Dr. Magan, let me tell you a story."

"Go on," replied Dr. Magan.

"I was called to Hinsdale one day to operate on a woman who was afflicted with an abdominal cancer. Only a few moments sufficed, after we began the work, to satisfy me that surgical aid was futile. I told the nurses and the sick woman's people that we were powerless. After leaving the operating room I came along the same path we are treading today. Soon I was aware that someone was following me with hurried step. I turned to see David Paulson rushing after me.

"He caught me by the arm and said 'Dr. Martin, what about that poor woman?'

"I told him that nothing could be done for her."

"What did David say to that?" asked Dr. Magan.

"He said something that has been with me through life. He said, 'Well, it may be you're right. Humanly speaking I suppose you are, but after all, Franklin Martin, there's a God in heaven—a God in heaven—a God in heaven. That God can raise people up when you and I fail.' Then he turned and rushed back to the sanitarium."

Dr. Magan was curious and asked him how the patient fared after that. Dr. Martin continued:

"Months passed away, and one day this woman whom I had pronounced hopeless walked into my office in Chicago. At first I didn't recognize her. When I did, she told me this story:

" 'After you operated on me that day I was lying on my bed still partially under the influence of the anesthetic. I heard my relatives saying that Dr. Martin had told them I could not live. A horror of great darkness filled my soul. I felt I could not go and leave my husband and children, who needed me so badly. Soon I heard the voice of David Paulson praying. He seemed to be talking with God about me and telling his Father in heaven how greatly my family needed me. I lay very still, and the prayer continued. It went on and on and on. Then it was that a great peace filled my soul. I knew that there was one man who could talk with God most intimately and whose heart longings God heard. That is why I'm alive today.'

"That was her story," said Dr. Martin.

"Do you know she was entirely cured, Doctor?"

"Oh, yes, I know. I examined her subsequently in my office and found no trace of malignancy, and as far as I know she is alive today. Talk about miracles! I think we still have them."

"Yes," Dr. Magan agreed, "that story sounds like Bible times."

"Dr. Magan, let me tell you two things. If anyone else in all the world had talked to me after David Paulson's manner, I would have set him down at once as a fanatic and a visionary religionist, but it was never so with David Paulson. Somehow or other when that man spoke a feeling amounting to certain knowledge took possession of my soul. I felt that I was in the presence of one to whom God was a real, living, personal Friend and confidant. It was ever thus."

"But, Dr. Martin, you were about to tell me something else you wanted to say."

"Oh, yes. The Hinsdale Sanitarium is a good place. Dr. Mary Paulson, a talented woman, who is considered one of the best woman diagnosticians in Chicago, and her nurses, have done great things. But when all is said and done, many a soul who came to the Hinsdale Sanitarium for help would be under the sod today were it not for David Paulson's prayers."

That brief visit with Dr. Franklin H. Martin remained in Dr. Magan's memory through the years. Dr.

Magan was later called to connect with the College of Medical Evangelists in Loma Linda and Los Angeles California. As president of the institution Dr. Magan was largely responsible for bringing the school, the only one of its kind in the United States, to the attention and approval of the highest medical authorities in this country. It was at the dedication of the David Paulson Memorial Hall in Los Angeles, with Dr. Martin as guest speaker, that Dr. Magan told this story I have just related.

There were many other cases of healing in the Hinsdale Sanitarium in those days, but such prayers were always offered privately in the sickroom. Never was there a public demonstration of prayer for the sick.

There was one more case of healing I would like to record. A man from Nebraska brought his wife to the sanitarium for treatment for pernicious anemia. The laboratory tests showed that her blood was almost as thin as water. The weeks were passing, with no sign of improvement. When Dr. Paulson felt that the end was near he telegraphed her husband to come at once. It was agreed there was no hope from a human standpoint.

When Dr. Mary asked her patient whether there was anything she had to say, she feebly responded with only one word, "Pray." Dr. David and Dr. Mary knelt at her bedside and humbly and earnestly committed this dying woman to God's restoring power for recovery if it was His will. From that hour she began to improve, and in three months went home a comparatively well woman. A letter from her husband some time later said that his wife was as well as ever and had gained fifty pounds. I knew this woman personally and saw the gradual change in her condition as the weeks went by.

Dr. Paulson often said that if Providence helped us to establish the Hinsdale Sanitarium (and he never doubted that), then why couldn't the Lord help the sick people to get well there? Many patients carry gratitude to God in their hearts today because Dr. Paulson prayed for them back there.

These experiences yield an intimate insight into David Paulson's private prayer life. His faith in God was simple and sincere. It was not a mere emotion of the mind, but a recognition of things as they actually exist. He was able to recommend the sick to the great Creator and Healer of men and cooperate intelligently with Him.

With David Paulson prayer was a habit in which he indulged more often than in his daily food. It helped him to fulfill his vow to God.

CHAPTER SEVENTEEN

A Vow to God Fulfilled

David's promise to God when a mere lad became the ruling motive of his entire life. He went all the way. Like the Master, he went about doing good and healing diseases.

He secured a medical education, the best obtainable in those days. Then he was able to fulfill his great ambition in life—to be a medical missionary.

He went into the heart of Chicago's slums, where he spent five years ministering to the bodies and souls of the denizens of the underworld. He preached Christ through his life.

He went from Chicago to Hinsdale, Illinois, and singlehanded, with an empty pocketbook, but with strong faith, built a sanitarium for the sick of earth.

When his health failed he had four resident physicians and a large number of visiting physicians on the medical staff of the Hinsdale Sanitarium, an accredited nurses' training school, with more than a hundred student nurses in training continuously, some three hundred employees in all, and a hospital building costing over seven hundred thousand dollars, which he had built year by year with prayers and tears. He also conducted a visiting nurses' extension department, giving student nurses experience in caring for the poor and unfortunate of Chicago, and affording them experience in soul winning at the Life Boat Home for Girls, which he had established in Hinsdale.

Aside from his responsibilities in connection with the sanitarium, he was frequently called to lecture in churches, high schools, and various organizations for the betterment of humanity.

He was never strong physically, and his brain pushed his body beyond endurance. At the earnest request of his family and friends he spent the winter of 1913-14 in old Mexico with his brother Julius.

During that winter his mind never relaxed. As his secretary, I was flooded with letters, articles for publication, materials for conventions, schools of health, and all sorts of promotion ideas for the advancement of the work—all written in his own hand. In the early spring of 1914 he returned to the States not much bettered from a winter in the delightful climate of Mexico, and plunged into a heavy program.

Two years later, in 1916, after a two days' lecture engagement in another State the doctor returned with a high fever.

It was then he thought of the future of the Hinsdale Sanitarium. His brother Julius had been driven out of Mexico during the revolution of 1914. He was obliged to leave a large and prosperous business to his 150 Mexican employees. Julius was persuaded to take over the management of the Hinsdale Sanitarium and was already on the premises. With the responsibility of the sanitarium in capable hands, David, then very ill, seemed to carry no further concern about the work at Hinsdale that he had so courageously established.

After a few weeks at home he improved, but the fever never left him. He sought relief by trying different climates. At Dr. Magan's urgent request he spent a month in the Madison Sanitarium near Nashville, Tennessee. Another month he sojourned in the Boulder, Colorado, Sanitarium. There the high altitude seemed to improve him for a time, but he soon had to return to Hinsdale, no better than when he left.

One day in September, 1916, he said to his wife, "Mamie, I am thinking of that pure, fresh air in Asheville, North Carolina, and the glorious sunshine up there in the mountains. If I were there, I think I would get well."

"David, if you want to go to Asheville, I'll take you there at once."

"Yes, Mamie, I would like to go."

Preparations were made immediately for the trip. Taken by ambulance from Hinsdale, seventeen miles of careful driving brought him to the railroad station in Chicago. There on his stretcher he was lifted carefully through the car window and into his drawing room. An official of the railroad company made the trip with him to make sure that everything was done for his comfort. Dr. Mary never left his side.

They had to transfer en route, and while he was being carried from the train he passed the giant locomotive that had brought him safely thus far. The big, burly engineer in his visor cap and blue overalls stood by his cab.

"Hi, Doctor! Did I give you a smooth ride?" he shouted.

David was unable to answer, but his attendant replied, "Yes, chief; I see by the tears in his eyes that the doctor wants to thank you."

"I had orders not to jerk this train while you were on it," called the engineer as they passed on.

So he traveled in ease, without even a jolt of the train. Not much like the jerky, jolty ride he took on the little train across the Dakota prairies twenty-eight years before. That was when he left home to get an education and to fulfill his vow to God to give his life for suffering humanity.

His life had been a short, colorful one. In reviewing it, we were reminded of that night years before when he and Mamie stood on the bridge over the Kalamazoo River in Battle Creek, Michigan, facing the future together. They talked about the beauty of the river as it sparkled in the moonlight, tumbling over the rocks and boulders in its path. David wondered then whether his life would be beset with trials—rocks of difficulty across his path. How true a picture it was of what was to be!

Looking into the mirror of his life, we find there many poignant moments. These were met and conquered by his faith and prayer, which drew him nearer, ever nearer to the realization of his partnership with God.

His vow had now been accomplished, and he was ready for whatever the Lord had next for him. It was the pattern he had followed all his life.

Many precious promises sustained David Paulson during those months of suffering from the fever. He spoke of these as he gained confidence and courage in the Lord.

"When we are in deep trouble we want to get rid of it speedily, but only God knows when we have had enough. I wanted to get rid of my fever, and get well, but then there came to my mind the Master's prayer when He was in deep trouble: 'Father, if thou be willing, remove this cup from me: nevertheless not my will, but thine, be done' (Luke 22:42). I had a precious experience when I was able to pray that prayer from my heart. Luke says that when Christ prayed that prayer an angel came and strengthened Him. I verily believe one came to strengthen me.

"I am glad I can today put my finger on Psalms 119:75 and say from my heart: 'I know, Lord, that thy judgments are right, and that thou in faithfulness hast afflicted me.' "

In a little mountain cabin, the place he longed for in Asheville, North Carolina, the flood of life was fast ebbing away. News of his serious illness was spreading over the country. Dr. Magan left his important work and sped across the country to pass the closing days of David Paulson's life with him, giving him encouragement with his counsel and prayers.

Dr. Paulson left no great estate for his heirs; in fact, he made no plans for future ease and comfort. He was always giving not only of his life energy but also of his means. Often he would say, "If I help others in need, the Lord will take care of me when I need help." He never trusted the Lord in vain.

A wealthy businessman nearly two thousand miles away heard the news that David Paulson was seriously ill, and rushed to his bedside, arriving just an hour before the doctor passed away on Sunday afternoon,

Dr. Paulson Hall, College of Medical Evangelists.

October 15, 1916. That man, desirous of doing something for the doctor who had enriched his life, took charge of the entire financial responsibilities incident to his death, the comfort of his party, transportation, and all expenses. He said, "Dr. Paulson has done more for me than any man on earth. What little I can do now is nothing." That man was W. K. Kellogg, the Battle Creek cereal manufacturer.

Today Dr. Paulson is remembered by thousands as an outstanding pioneer in medical missionary work. The Hinsdale Sanitarium, which he founded, a near-million-dollar institution at his death, has now been rebuilt at a cost of three and a half million with Federal and State support. Its magnificent five-story hospital and the David Paulson Memorial Hall in Los Angeles, belonging to the College of Medical Evangelists, both stand as monuments to his life.

His greatest monument, however, is the hundreds of medical missionary doctors and nurses who were his students and who today are blessing humanity, many of whom have served the Master in foreign lands.

David Paulson was a true American in spirit and in practice. He believed in the principles of freedom and in the brotherhood of man, giving his entire life for the betterment of humanity.

It wasn't so much what he attained in life that made him great, according to material standards, as it was his noble, unselfish spirit that reached down into the physical and spiritual needs of mankind. His secret of success was the fact that he had discovered and grasped the highest Source of power in the world pledged to man's rehabilitation and salvation.

He had to struggle against physical handicaps, but he lived two lives in one in the brief forty-eight years allotted him. His life was cut short, but his influence has grown brighter and brighter as the years have passed by. After his death his friend and colleague, Dr. Franklin H. Martin, founder of the American College of Surgeons, sent the following beautiful tribute, which was published in the *Life Boat*.

"His inspired and inspiring life, his clear vision, his irresistible enthusiasm for the promulgation of truth, his wise counsel, his ability to impart knowledge, his love for the outcast, the downhearted and neglected of earth, all combine to make David Paulson one of God's noblemen."

At this early morning hour, as I trace these last few lines of the story of a great man of faith, I look to the West, over the vast Pacific Ocean, still asleep under the gray mantle of night. But as I turn to the East I can see the first rays of dawn breaking over the bay, setting it aglow with the golden light of hope. So we leave David in the hands of the Sun of Righteousness, who has arisen with healing in His wings and conquered the dark night of sin and the grave, for him, for you, and for me.